And the Two Became One

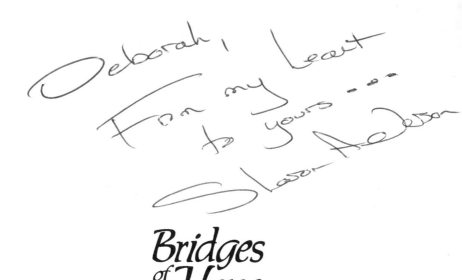

Plus

*Deborah,
From my heart
to yours . . .
Sharon A. Jetson*

Bridges of Hope

PUBLISHING

And the Two Became One Plus

An Upfront Look at Today's Blended Family

Sharon Anderson

AND THE TWO BECAME ONE PLUS —
AN UPFRONT LOOK AT TODAY'S BLENDED FAMILY

Copyright © 1994 by Sharon Anderson
Printed in the United States of America

"Scripture taken from the HOLY BIBLE, NEW INTERNATIONAL VERSION. Copyright © 1973, 1978, 1984 by International Bible Society. Used by permission of Zondervan Publishing House."

Published by: Bridges of Hope Publishers
                 So. Easton, Massachusetts

Printed by: Burgess Printing Company

Library of Congress Catalog Number: 94-96253

ISBN: 0-9642838-0-8

Front Cover Design by: Baird Design

Front Cover Photo by: John Ventresco

To contact Sharon Anderson about "BLENDED FAMILY SEMINARS" write, Bridges of Hope Ministries, P.O. Box 407, So. Easton, MA 02375 or call (508) 583-1555.

Cover Photo (left to right):
Katy, Brad, Christy, Brian, Karl, Amy, Sharon, and Rachel Anderson

8 7 6 5 4 3 2 1

This book is lovingly dedicated to

My husband, Karl

whose silent strength I value

and

My children,

Katy, Amy, Brian, Rachel, Christy, Bradley

whose individuality I treasure

Acknowledgements

Though I am the author of this book and most of its content is written out of my own experience and perspective, I am in debt to a number of individuals who have provided the emotional, technical, and financial support needed for a project, such as this, to be completed. I owe special thanks to...

My husband, Karl and children, Katy, Amy, Brian, Rachel, Christy, and Brad, who prayed every night for the past four years that "Mom's book would get published."

My mother, Sally Jo Harff, who never stopped whispering the words, "You can do it."

My brother and his wife, Bob and Ellyn Patterson, who signed on to this dream emotionally from Day One.

My friends, John and Sonnie Dreystadt, for their confidence in me and the tangible ways in which they expressed it.

My assistant, Jill Hutchinson, for her gracious manner and tireless commitment to detail.

My graphic artist, Richard Baird, for his creative gifts, guidance, and advice.

My aunt, Mary Lou Patterson, and my brother-in-law, Paul Anderson for their editing assistance and the candid way in which they "cleaned" up my act.

From the Author...

This is a story about an unmistakably common, yet remarkably uncommon family. It is a chronicle of their undeniably ordinary, yet amazingly unordinary journey. They are, what is known as, a "blended" or "ready-made" family. They are comprised of eight unique individuals, who, over the past twelve years, have made a love connection with one another.

Though their numbers, names, and natures may be different from other blended families, their experience has been quite similar. They have wrestled with the same see-saw of emotions; they have cried the same tears of pain; and they have waded through the same sea of adjustment. The particulars of their pilgrimage is detailed through the most intimate of eyes — mine. I am the wife and mother of this colorful brood.

The details of our journey have not been watered down or color-coated. I paint a true-to-life picture of life in the blended lane. I also identify a number of blended principles which have the potential to bring about authentic bonding in a blended home.

But most important of all, I offer hope. A personal, yet all-encompassing hope that is found in God's power to change people, attitudes and situations. The kind of hope that comes from watching God transform your life and home in ways you never thought possible.

It is the confidence that believes that even when you don't have all the answers to the problems of blended life, there is "Someone" beside you that does. And it is the assurance that understands that even though you are powerless to bring love into your tension-filled relationships, you are in the hands of the "One" who is not.

I offer this hope humbly and with thanks to the "One" responsible for the "oneness" we now enjoy.

Table of Contents

Introduction

My own story:

I was divorced in 1979. I had two children, a home, and a challenging job in a cosmetic company in Minneapolis. During a vacation on the East Coast, the home of my childhood, I met my future husband, Karl. He, too, had been divorced in 1979 and was raising three children as well as running a successful manufacturing business.

After a brief courtship, we married in 1982. The names and ages of our children were Katy—13, Amy—11, Brian—7, Rachel—6 and Christy—5! I realized very quickly that this territory was not for the emotionally weak or easily defeated. No one could have ever prepared me for the challenges ahead. Solomon, for all his wisdom could not have foreseen the multitude of problems we would face, not once in a while, but on a daily basis. Still worse, these waters for the most part were largely uncharted...very little had been written on how to successfully blend families.

Ground rules needed to be established immediately for the sake of everyone, and our commitment to see our family grow together needed to be kept foremost in our minds at all times (one can lose this quickly if not extremely careful). I decided to keep a journal of our progress, so throughout this book you will see my open, honest reactions to the mountains and valleys on that journey.

I will offer practical advice on ways to bring about authentic bonding as well as warnings of the potential pitfalls that lead to division in the ranks. I will not be dispensing magical formulas or written guarantees. Beginning again in marriage with children is, at best, a daring venture but an attainable one. I must warn you that if you are serious about your commitment, you are going to work harder than you ever thought possible.

This region of family life is not for those who want to "do their own thing". These children need love, support, time, and discipline. This is not an easy task. There will be times when you will wonder why you ever took on this enormous responsibility, but let me assure you that lo and behold a deeper love can emerge than you ever thought possible. This is when yours and mine become "ours", and you are a family in the deepest sense.

It is my honest conviction that we would have never been able to blend our families as well as we have without the help of God. He is truly in the business of bringing healing and wholeness into our daily lives. If I believe one thing about the past twelve years, it is this: God is a God of new beginnings. We have experienced His touch in our home and you can in yours as well.

Let me share a portion of a letter written to our family by our daughter, Amy, as she left for college:

To my dear family,
    Well, this is it! I'm off to college. I'm excited for what is about to happen in my life yet sad for everything I will miss from not being around all of you on a daily basis. While I was clearing out my room and thinking of all that has transpired over the course of many years, the bonding that has occurred between each of us is tremendous! I hope you all know exactly what each and everyone of you mean to me. No one could ever have asked for a nicer family than I've got. I thank God for all of you because I really am blessed. I love you all very much!
                                        Amy

Chapter 1

Keep A Close Relationship
With Your Spouse

"Thank you for the happiest year I've ever had...may the rest of our lives be as good as we have had together already."

Karl

I first came to know Karl briefly while we attended the same church some years ago. Since we were both married at the time and didn't run in the same social circles, we were virtual strangers when we met again in 1980. It was while I was living in Minneapolis that I heard about his marital struggles and impending divorce. The dissolution of his marriage was to be a long process which would eventually take three years to settle.

It was during a vacation trip to the East Coast that I became reacquainted with him through mutual friends. Over dinner one evening, we shared for hours the emotional sagas of our divorces as well as our concerns about being single parents. It was so good to talk with someone who was travelling the same road and grappling with the same uncertainties of the future. Since Karl's divorce was not yet final, we never spoke again until the following summer when I once again returned to New England. This time our families spent a day together on Cape Cod with his closest friends and, as before, we parted with no promise of any future.

It wasn't until eight months later when his settlement was final that I received a phone call from him announcing his desire to see me again. In May of 1982, I flew to Boston for a "weekend date"! Since I was there for such a short time, we spent every waking hour together. We went to the movies, walked along the ocean, and ate at wonderful Boston restaurants. It was during an afternoon at an old fishing village by the sea that he held my hand for the first time as we browsed through the quaint shops on the pier. I remember every detail as if it were yesterday, since those small acts of affection take on special meaning as you emerge from months of despair, sadness, and loneliness. I have come to realize that regardless of the circumstances, whether by death or divorce, intimate moments such as this become particularly meaningful.

We were both surprised to see how strong our feelings were after such a short time. After I returned to Minneapolis, we continued our courtship "by phone"! We kept the phone company in business since we spoke each night for at least one to two hours. We planned another "date" in Boston the following month and this time our talks included our future together and the definite conclusion that neither of us were interested in going on without the other. My journal confirms this when I wrote, *"I'm miserable without him...life isn't the same...I don't even enjoy the things I used to...all I can think of is being together all the time."* I was in love and so was he! As soon as I returned to Minneapolis, a card arrived in the mail that read, "Since you left, I can't eat and I can't sleep...please come back and bring a pizza and a pillow with you!" In it he wrote, "Sharon, you have changed my life so much for the better that I have to keep pinching myself to see if I'm just having a fantastic dream...the future looks so wonderful sharing my life with you and you with me that it blows my mind ...I know we can make life so beautiful together that no matter what comes along to disrupt, we will be happy...I want nothing but the best for us and our children." We both had a real peace that God had brought us together and constantly thanked Him for this new beginning.

Our wedding date was set for early fall and it was decided that I would immediately put my house on the market and make preparations for an August move. We wanted my children to become established in their new school system at the beginning of the fall semester. The days flew by as we planned the details of my move, our wedding, and the weeks that would follow. At the end of August, Karl flew out to help me load my entire house into one large Ryder truck. Leaving my extended family was especially difficult for me. As thrilled as I was about my marriage to Karl, I cried for hours as we drove out of Minneapolis. My mother and I had always shared such a special relationship that I knew how much I would miss seeing and talking to her on a daily basis.

Little did I know after I arrived in Boston what each new day would bring. And as excited as Karl and I were about our new life together, it was hard to dismiss the look of horror on some of our children's faces at the mere thought that we were actually going to go through with this crazy idea. Like "love-sick" teenagers (that described us well), we were confident that we would be able to make this marriage work!

October 2 was a glorious autumn day in New England and the entire family worked for hours getting our Tyrolean mansion (by that I mean we have 16 rooms, 6 bedrooms and 4 bathrooms!) ready for our quiet ceremony with close friends and family. My mother, who was to be matron of honor, had arrived earlier in the week so she also assisted in all the last minute preparations. It was a hubbub of activity as the house was rearranged to seat fifty guests. The florist decorated in gentle peach hues and the caterer set up for a lovely buffet. Dresses were ironed, showers were taken, hairdo's were set, suitcases were packed, and even the dog was washed as evening approached.

The ceremony had been carefully planned to include crisp entrances and attentive participants. Of course, what should happen and what does happen is often an entirely different matter. For us, it would be a slight delay in our arrival when the man who had been designated to run the music couldn't figure out how to start "Bach" (nerves I guess) and the constant fidgeting of our younger children whenever the minister spoke. Regardless of these interruptions, however, this was a very special moment for us both as each of our children stood with us and witnessed the vows we were making to each other. At that moment, a new chapter in our lives had just begun and its opening line read, "And the 'two' became 'one' plus 'five'!"

Our honeymoon plans included spending five nights at different quaint New England Country Inns. One of our favorites was the Von Trapp Inn (of the Sound of Music legend) in Stowe, Vermont. The view resembled the most picturesque of postcards. What wonderful memories we have of those five days.

Meanwhile, back at the ranch, my mother had been left in charge of our children. It took her no time at all to lay down her hard and fast rules of eating whatever you wanted (they had brownies for breakfast), going to bed when the spirit moved (midnight was no problem), and missing school if you felt like it (can you imagine the excuse she used on the absence note)! She was an instant hit with all the kids! We were all certainly in for an enormous adjustment when the reality of rules, homework, and domestic responsibility came to bear after living with "Auntie Mame" for a week! So with one foot in front of the other, our family began its own "run for the roses".

As you begin the blending process, it is crucial that your children witness your commitment to each other on a daily basis. From the day that you announce your wedding plans to the months following the "I do's", each one of your children will struggle with how they will fit into this new home order. As we listened to their everyday comments, two non-verbal questions came out loudly and clearly. They were "Am I wanted here?" and "Will this marriage end, too?"

Based on this reality, we sat around our dining room table with all five children during our first week together to set down two very important ground rules. The first was to assure them that this marriage was forever or until one of us died. They could count on it...we were here for the long haul. Secondly, we would not allow them to come between us. We would be working as a team in all matters that pertained to them individually and to our overall home life. The words and sentiment behind "You will not be allowed to come between us" are certainly easy to feel and say, but living it out on a day by day basis is another story. Let me share with you a very honest, candid view of my early feelings as found in my journal:

> *"On one of our first days together, I had the hardest time. I cried most of the day and felt almost overwhelmed by the enormous responsibility I had taken on. I was extremely exasperated with Karl's kids as well as completely sorry I had uprooted my children to come here. As the day progressed, I got worse and the anger, bitterness and frustration mounted. After dinner Karl and I went for a walk which proved to be a real time of honest sharing both of our own feelings and the feelings we had toward each others children...in the end we came up with some good compromises for us both."*

I understand now, more than ever, how important it was for our relationship to remain paramount as we balanced the priorities of our new life together. These incidents, such as the one I have just recalled, would continue for months and, in some areas, for years; it was crucial that we continually nurtured our marriage. As I told Karl, "even when I am at my worst with adjustments, I never doubt my love for you...I think it is the fact that I love you so much that keeps me going through difficult times." In other words, our relationship was the "Gator-Ade" we would both need as we daily ran laps of discouragement, dejection, and heartache.

In order to foster our alliance, we regularly got away from the clamor and pressures of our new home. We went out to dinner, saw a movie, or did some of the things we enjoyed while dating. And at least once every six months, we found someone to watch our children and we took off for a "two-day" vacation. It doesn't sound like a very long time but, believe me, those 48 hours were enough for our intimacy to be rekindled, our strength renewed, and our emotional communion revitalized. Walking away from the hassles of everyday living does wonders for your marriage relationship and it gives your children an opportunity to appreciate your presence in their lives. Potentially speaking, a break from each other can be very therapeutic!

Another facet of a blended marriage that takes a perpetual beating is your "affaire d'amour" (romantic intrigue). The validity of this statement comes from the fact that you are seldom alone and when you are, you are exhausted! Due to the tremendous demands on each of you, the brief love affair you once enjoyed (your honeymoon) can easily lose its flavor. The essence of this truth is captured in these words from my journal, "*as far as my relationship with Karl goes, it's terrific. I really do love him and he is so good to me in all respects. He is gentle, kind and good and I constantly thank God for him. I*

23

enjoy his company very much and love my quiet times with him (which are very few)!"

You see, when you enter marriage for the first time, your hours together are basically uninterrupted. No little ones are asking to sleep with you at all hours of the night and no adolescents are asking you "what you are doing" when your door is locked! When the nuptial knot includes ready-made children, however, these invasions of privacy can become a regular occurrence. We were beginning to think we lived with spies when one of them went as far as to inquire, "Why do you have candles lit in your room in the middle of the night!" "What candles?" we asked!

For us, the luxury of spontaneous "fraternizing" was made quite impossible with five children, so we learned to make the most of any romantic free-time. But even the best of plans are open to surprises. I remember one such occasion when all of the children were going to be out of the house for the entire evening. As soon as the last one left, we shut off every light in the house (so even our friends would not stop by), lit the candles, turned on the stereo and proceeded to enjoy the "quiet" (if you understand what I mean)! After only twenty minutes, someone started knocking and ringing our door bell without stopping for what seemed to be an eternity! When I finally answered the door (we were in total shock), our fifteen-year-old son said, "Mom, what's wrong? Why didn't you answer the door? Has there been a power outage?" It never occurred to him that his Dad and I had a life outside of him and his sisters.

The dense jungle of emotions within a blended family is full of ensnaring traps that threaten to choke the very life out of your marriage relationship. One such pitfall is the tendency to blame your partner for their child's behavior. This tactic comes naturally when your new child's entire demeanor tells you they are less than thrilled about your presence in their life. It is especially true when their darts of hostility hit the bull's-eye of your heart with stinging accuracy. Many times as I reached the pinnacle of frustration, it was my husband, not my new children who took the first blow as my verbal punching bag. My language often suggested that he was somehow responsible for their every word and action.

My husband, on the other hand, never held me accountable in any way for the conduct of my children. He kept our relationships distinctly separate and dealt with each of us according to our own merits and inadequacies. Even when our own marriage saw stormy weather, he was careful not to take his feelings of unfulfillment out on my children. By doing this, Karl continually strengthened the stabilization of our home. Continual accusations can have a crippling effect on your marriage if they become a part of everyday communication. Your home can become more like a harsh courtroom than a haven of harmony. In order to avoid adding unnecessary burden to your budding relationship, refrain from transferring blame from your child to your spouse. Deliver your subpoenas of guilt to the appropriate parties and make it a point to keep short accounts.

Other pitfalls to be experienced in the "blended jungle" is the tendency to put your marriage relationship on the back burner after hearing your child say, "You're never just with me anymore." The guilt you once carried while being single can easily be carried over into your new life. Don't underestimate the tremendous pull you will feel in this area. You are dealing with jealousy and it can be a powerful tool within your child's hand to drive a wedge between you and your spouse. It happens and it is devastating. Now, of course, the goal is always balance within your new family but be careful not to be manipulated into neglecting your own mate in order to appease the demands of a child in transition.

In his book, <u>Tyranny of the Urgent</u>, Charles Hummel says that it is easy "to let the urgent take the place of the important in your life." This is especially true of blended parents as they daily face a full docket of responsibilities. Don't let this happen to you...take time for each other. Let the children see how close you are.

This might be intimidating to them at first, but it can provide a real sense of confidence in your "marriage-ability" as the months and years go by. While pulling into the driveway one day with our daughter, Christy, she observed the warmth displayed by my husband as he greeted me with a smile and a wave. Immediately, she asked, "You really love him, don't you?" "Yes, I do," was my reply. Pausing a moment, she responded, "That makes me feel so good inside." You see, our closeness was no longer a threat but a source of comfort. Our children were experiencing "security" in action.

Chapter 2

Be Kind To Those Children

"This card is to a mother I'll never forget...she has been very kind to me through the years (all eight of them)!"

Brian

Right before my marriage to Karl, I read a quote from Florence Pauls, a stepmother and educator. It added enormous perspective to my new role as an "assumable" parent.

"Be kind to those children. You may not be able to love them the way you would your own, although sometimes you can, but they are so vulnerable. They haven't learned yet even how to handle the problems of just living. They have a right as children to be treated with great gentleness but also firmness. If you don't believe you can behave in this way, you just don't have any right to become one of their parents. When you marry that guy or gal, you marry that person's children, too — you really do. You'd better think it through before you take it on."

I found these words of caution especially helpful since I realized quickly that the magic of being carried across the threshold did not anoint me with feelings of love toward my new children. You see, we had spent very little time together and what quality hours we did share were masked by the fact that everyone was on their best behavior. Personally speaking, it was very important for me to receive an approval grade from Karl's children while we were dating, so I was careful to respond with the humbleness of Mother Teresa, the laughter of Lucille Ball, and the sweetness of Shirley Temple whenever we interacted. (And of course, the sex appeal of Marilyn Monroe for Karl!) They, too, were constantly sporting their best behavior for their father's sake and often behaved in a way that resembled china dolls.

The reality of living would not take form until we daily faced the peculiar quirks of our different personalities. After only two weeks together, it was as if we received an anonymous telegram that read, "Welcome to the Real World." The polite expressions became honest words, the smiling faces began to admit other emotions, and normal conduct took the place of flawless etiquette as we began to deal with the dirt and grime of everyday living. We never knew the luxury of relying upon warm-hearted, affectionate feelings when the going got tough. Those inner stirrings would take years to establish, and even my sincere craving for instant attachment would prove to be pure fantasy.

In order to grapple with everyday struggles, I learned, as never before, the true meaning of the courtesy "kindness". Its action implies taking an interest in, sympathizing with, feeling for, treating well, giving comfort and assisting. These everyday acts of hospitality were responses to which I could relate with on a moment by moment basis. In regard to the children, I knew I *could* take an interest in their Girl Scout activities or in their new cheer for the big game; I knew I *could* sympathize with their disappointment at not making the team or not getting the part they wanted in the class play; I knew I *could* feel for their insecurity in relating with their peers or with their sensitivity toward weight and face problems; I knew I *could* give them comfort when they faced the pain of exclusion by friends. I knew I *could* assist them when they needed help with a school project or with choosing a new outfit for an upcoming activity. All of these positive pieces of caring were within my reach when the word "love" hadn't yet been added to my emotional vocabulary. They were attainable and didn't require years of practice. They gave me a target to shoot for — something concrete and achievable.

When two families first come together, the parents are often bombarded with hostile comparisons to a former lifestyle. Complaints such as, "we never did it that way before" or icy glares that read, "I can do it myself...I don't need your help" can feel like a knock-out punch. If you hear enough of them in a given week, you begin to know the feeling of being "down for the count". Having a dictionary of attitudes stapled on the bulletin board of your mind can help you react, in a positive rather than a negative way to these "defense mechanisms" of your children. These practical means of building affection helped me keep my new children's best interests at heart in the midst of these SCUD attacks. These emotional pricks are painful, to say the least, but *don't be black-mailed into changing who you are or your way of doing things to accommodate children at a turning point in their lives.* You need to be sensitive to individual struggles, of course, but *do not try and imitate their past.* This futile attempt will only postpone your own voyage toward a new family life.

Early in our marriage, I adopted a personal rule which was played out daily (even hourly) as I began to respond to the personal challenges, attitudes and habits of my new brood. It was to *"treat these children exactly the way I would want my natural children treated if they did not live with me."* I cannot tell you how often my initial reaction was changed when this vow flashed before my eyes. It slowed me down; it made me weigh my words more carefully; it helped me remember the losses and adjustment these children had already experienced in their young lives. It did not change the rules or bound-aries within our home, but it did alter the way verbal corrections were delivered and the way punishments were meted out.

You see, these children are not responsible for the death or divorce of a parent. If there is anything such as an innocent party, it is these vulnerable young people. At this point, they are worthy of the label "Handle With Care" as they recover from loss, sadness, and pain. They deserve parents who will champion their cause with a tender touch.

Often times, though, we think the imperative "Be kind to those children!" really means "Go easy on those children". Well, it doesn't. I have taken great pains to overemphasize the importance of showing good will and charity to your new children, but I, in no way, mean to imply letting them enjoy "self-rule". It is important they be given rules and responsibilities within your new home, and they be made accountable for their actions. This not only builds character and self-worth, but also instills security and a sense of normalcy for your new child. Your expectations can make them feel that they are an important part of your new team.

An example of this blending law took place immediately after we were married when Karl and I made the decree that every child had to do their part to keep our home in shape. Thus, every Saturday, they would be expected to clean their own rooms as well as complete assigned chores. They were not allowed to leave the house unless all their tasks were completed. A note from my journal tells you up front exactly how one of my daughters felt about this new rule. *"She resented being told to do anything since she had been pretty much doing her own thing for the past three years."* There was heavy grumbling from each of them at the beginning as they learned to fulfill the various responsibilities of keeping a house clean. They washed floors, cleaned bathrooms, dusted furniture, vacuumed carpets and ironed shirts. If you were to ask any of them at the time whether they appreciated our firmness in this or other areas, their answer, no doubt, would have been a flat-out *"No"*!

31

My husband and I made it a point of working alongside them each week. If you remember, I wrote in the introduction that "this region of family life is not for those who want to 'do their own thing'. These children need love, support, time, and discipline." How true this was of the Saturday mornings in our home. It would have been easy for Karl and I to take off and enjoy a day together and let our minors fend for themselves. But the truth is they needed our supervision. We were quick to compliment those jobs well done and were equally as critical when their efforts lacked, should I say, elbow grease. Each of them can well remember hearing the order, "Do it again until it is done right!", on more than one occasion. These were difficult days for each of us as we learned to adjust to both the good and bad of each other's past lifestyle. But I believe it was those silent acts of kindness, such as our time and presence, that grafted new skin to the face of our changing relationships. By the way, some of these very same young people made money through college cleaning houses!

Though my decision to "treat my new children exactly the same way I would want my natural children treated if they did not live with me" was indeed a conscious one, I must confess that I did not obey my own rule at every turn. At times, I was able to retreat for the moment and rethink my response but at other moments, my short temper and bad humor were off and running and heading full speed ahead at these fractured targets.

I recall two separate occasions when neither my husband nor I would have received honors for the way we handled the inevitable blunders of our children. The first happened during our second month of marriage when one of Karl's daughters made an off-the-cuff remark about what a "nuisance" my children were in her life. My frame of mind was such that her brutal frankness was more than I could handle. My initial hurt quickly turned to total outrage. For three days, I acted as if she didn't even exist. My silence was deadening — she had been shut out and she knew it. This must have been a very lonely feeling for a teenager seeking shelter in the arms of a new mother. In essence, I had let her wonder if her honesty had destroyed the new relationship we were beginning to enjoy. I was wrong. She deserved better. A confrontation should have taken place immediately (or at least after I had counted to ten) so I could have explained the reasons why her remark had been so difficult for me to hear and also to give her a chance to apologize (which she did).

The second incident still stirs feelings of sorrow and regret as I look back to that crisp, fall day when our children were loading leaves onto the back of our pick-up truck. As with all children, it wasn't long before they were clowning around and throwing each other off the flatbed. Brian pushed Rachel in such a way that when she landed on the pile of leaves the bone in her arm snapped right in half. Her instant panic manifested itself in blood-curdling screams and my husband, who isn't particularly calm in emergency situations, became totally unglued. He immediately began to verbally attack this poor young boy who was already beside himself with regret. Scared to death of his father's incensement, he ran into the woods. By the time I reached him, tears were rolling down his cheeks as he kept repeating, "I didn't mean it...I didn't mean to hurt her."

Even though my husband apologized when he returned from the hospital, I realized during the days that followed that extensive damage had been done to this already fragile relationship. With the help of a fiberglass cast, Rachel's arm mended itself in just a few short months, but the fracture within Brian's heart would take far longer to heal.

Another act of kindness you can award your new child is the freedom to enter into their new relationship with you in *their own time* and in *their own way*. Even though each of them stood at the altar with us, our children did not repeat the vows, Karl and I did. Committing themselves personally to their new parent would come at different times and at different places.

Relationships such as these cannot be forced. They evolve with time and require a great deal of perseverance. Expecting too much, too soon from these new "familyships" will only add to your already high frustration level. My oldest daughter, Katy, clearly remembers an incident years ago when we bumped into a group of people she knew as we were school shopping. Her noticeable pause told me she wasn't sure how to handle the upcoming introductions. I could almost hear her processing the question, "Should I call her Mom or Sharon?" I knew by the look on her face that she didn't want to hurt or offend me but certainly was not ready to typecast me as her mother. So I simply put out my hand and said, "Hi, I'm Sharon". I asked her recently what she remembers most about this encounter and she said there were two things. First, she didn't have to explain our situation...I had done it for her, and second, she knew at that moment, I wasn't going to push her. By not expecting more than she was willing to give, I gave her elbow room to discover the different aspects of who I was and what my presence could mean in her life. Now more than ever, these children need patience and compassion as they embrace their new family. I have found that it is through those small acts of warmth and kindness that a child is encouraged to issue a "bridge-building permit" to the new parent. In 1820, Thomas Chalmers penned these words, "Write your name in kindness, love, and mercy on the hearts of the thousands you meet, and it will become an indelible masterpiece none can ever forget." Today, please permit me to paraphrase these enduring words for you, a blended parent.

"Write your name in kindness, love, and mercy on the hearts of your new children, and it will become an indelible masterpiece they will never forget."
Sharon Anderson, 1994

Chapter 3

Communication — Your Ultimate Priority

"I appreciate all the talks we have. It's nice to know you are always there rooting for me. Thanks for being there when I needed you."

Christy

If I had to rank successful blending principles according to continuous priority, communication, without a doubt, would be at the top of my list. Without communication, the very hurdles you face each day would be like scaling Mount Everest without a rope. I would even go as far as to say that the lack of verbal give and take within your new home will eventually erode the very foundation you are attempting to build. These are strong words, I know, but they are, nonetheless, very true. Even though this book has been written for the sole purpose of addressing the unique needs of blended families, the art of communication pertains to all relationships and to all families. In fact, I believe the absence of meaningful dialogue within our homes is the main reason for the growing number of broken relationships within our society.

Many times, as I have interacted with members of a family in crisis, I found myself asking, "How did you get to this point...weren't you talking about these struggles?" The answers I heard most often fell into two basic categories — limited dialogue and deaf ears. Let me explain. The first and most prevalent answer was that these individuals really didn't talk to each other. Sure, they talked about everyday happenings such as the kids, the bills, and the lawn but they stayed away from sensitive issues such as their inner pain, frustrations, and fears. For a number of reasons, the dragon of personal emotions had been continually repressed and remained very guarded. Even when relational problems did occur, the "real" issues were never addressed. They were only swept under the carpet, the premise being that if you ignored it long enough, the problem would go away. Of course, it never did.

Then there were those individuals who had tried to communicate but whose words had fallen on deaf ears. Time and time again their attempts to open up and be vulnerable were met with the sounds of silence. No response eventually led to no interaction. These were sad, lonely, and unfulfilled people. Again, regardless of the reasons, faulty communication injures the overall well-being of any relationship. If these problems occur in so-called "whole" families, imagine the challenge facing those brave souls attempting to establish new family ties.

Years ago I attended an evening seminar at Bethel College in Minneapolis on "Stress", and in it the professor urged each of us to communicate openly and freely in order to keep our tension levels at a minimum. He left us with a quote that I have long since kept that speaks of the significance of good communication.

"A relationship is as good as its communication is clear. All good relationships have two-way communication. To love another as I love myself, is to protect or promote each others rights and responsibilities for equal communication, in equal conversation."

The type of communication to which I am referring must occur regularly between partners, between siblings and between parent and chiłd. This is not a weekly or even a monthly experience. Constant interaction must be part of one's daily routine. I noticed at the outset of my own marriage a tendency to hide my own feelings of frustration, anger, and disappointment from both my husband and my new children. The reasons for my self-defined mask was the fact that we had known each other for such a short time, and I wasn't at all sure how much honesty they could actually handle. And, since I didn't want to hurt anyone, I rationalized my silence as "keeping the peace at all costs" for the sake of our new family. But as I continued to honor my decision to "zipper my lip" on all inner struggles, fumes of resentment began to blow into the faces of the very people to whom I was trying to bond. You see, checking your changing emotions at the front door of your new home will only add to the tensions and pressures you will continually experience.

Please read this carefully because if you were sitting across from me right now, I would scream this message in your ear. *Personal lessons have taught me that these reasons, or for that matter, any reason to halt authentic communication, will ultimately do more harm than good.* Since my own personality seems to be incapable of squashing opinions, comments, or concerns for an indefinite period of time, it was not surprising to me when I reread these words from my early journal, *"One thing that has freed me up is to be honest and speak my piece when warranted — being real has helped me a lot."* It is curious that I used the word "freedom"; I must have felt like a prisoner within my own mind (and home) at times.

By opening up and owning up to what was going on inside me, I provided an example for which my children could follow. Depending on the backgrounds of both the parents and children before blending, communication will either come very naturally or will be viewed as a rather novel experience. In our home, for example, some of our children believed that their every thought should work like a gumball machine while others guarded their every word as if they were going to be displayed in the Smithsonian. In other words, the communication training they received in their previous environment will either help or hinder their adjustment toward their new siblings and parent.

I constantly reinforced *our need* to keep short accounts of irritations, infractions, and bitterness so as to ward off what I referred to earlier — resentment build-up, a definite hazard of the "Newlywed Family". My standard speech sounded something like this: "I cannot guess what you are thinking or feeling...I need you to tell me what is on your mind and in your heart...we can deal with anything we know about...if you keep it to yourself, *we are all in trouble!*" I stood on my soapbox and recited those words more times than I can count over the past twelve years, for I surely believed their silence to be my enemy.

I emphasized over and over again that, even if they felt their grievances were totally unsolvable (and often very repetitious), they had to be constantly "vented" for the sake of our family. Even my husband, who by his own admission is not a strong communicator, believed that only when issues and emotions were out in the open could we possibly begin to address the needs before us. For some of our children this was a relatively easy task because of their disposition and personality, but for others this would take enormous time and effort.

As the mother, I would constantly watch for the non-verbal signals that would tell me they were in trouble within themselves. You know, the look that says, "I hate the birds, the trees, our car, my clothes, your face!" If you have older children, you know that glare! My favorite place for these pow-wows (in other words, their date with Mom) was my living room but there was no sacred ground when it came to "letting it all hang out". In fact, I recall two separate occasions when my oldest daughter, Katy, and I were driving in the car, enjoying what seemed to be a casual conversation when all of a sudden, the audio sounded like a dramatic scene from *"Days of Our Lives"*. It didn't take a nuclear scientist to

41

conclude that just like a pregnant woman, we were about to deliver the verbal goods! The first time this happened, I pulled right into a church parking lot where the unloading began. Of course, it wasn't long before the tears flowed and honest communication started to take place. In the midst of this emotional drum roll, a man (I later found out it was the pastor) knocked on my car window to ask if there was anything he could do to help. We must have looked like two desperados about to commit "hara-kiri"! We both ended up laughing as we pulled away. The second incident was very similar, only this time, it was the local cemetery. To this day, whenever we pass those stones, Katy will always say, "Do you remember when...?" and we both laugh. You see, I have learned that when the tidal wave of dialogue appears, it is crucial that you ride the crest to shore. In other words, the surroundings are unimportant; the real issue is that the exchange take place. Try to be especially sensitive to those unplanned moments when your child unexpectedly drops their guard and allows you entrance into their "private think tank". Everything else can wait as you and your child take one step closer toward a deeper relationship.

Most of the time, though, these exchanges were well-planned by *Ma-Ma*! I waited until my hurting child was, for the most part, free of activities and then summoned them for a conference. Whenever I said, "I'd like to see you in the living room," all the other kids would go "Oooouuuu, you're in trouble now — Mom wants to talk." I tried to assure each of them of my love, concern, and desire to help. The rubber meets the road with such questions as, "I've been watching you for a few days now and something seems to be bothering you...are you having trouble here at home or at school...are things going poorly with your friends?" The take-off, at times, would be slow but once in flight, this encounter would almost always yield a frank and candid discussion of not only the initial complaint but of other emotions they had been holding in reserve. A freer, less burdened child and parent walked out of that room each time. Not that we had solved all their problems (or mine for that matter), but we had placed their concerns on the table and could now work toward possible solutions.

It is important to realize that the type of communication to which I am referring will only take place after your new child has become convinced that you really do care about them and that you can be trusted. Keep in mind that when you first marry their parent, their guard is up. They have built lots of walls of protection. In order for you to scale those weighty partitions, you are going to have to find ways of assuring them that you are "on their team."

I worked very hard during those early years to constantly affirm their worth in my eyes. I even went as far as sending cards to my teenagers at their high school telling them that I loved them and that I really cared about what was happening in their lives. I knew I had hit the spot when one would come through the door with a big smile and say, "Thanks, Mom, for the card. It was special." As I reflect over the past twelve years, I can see a direct relation between the amount of love shown and the amount of openness offered. In other words, the willingness of my new children to share the contents of their hearts came only after they began to believe in my love for them.

Not only is it imperative for children and their parents to communicate, it is equally as important for partners to do so as well. At the very beginning of our marriage, Karl and I made it a point each evening of going over each child's activities and any possible attitudes or behaviors that were of concern to either of us. This was also the time when I could say, "She is driving me crazy — why does she do this or why does she say that?", and he could say, "What am I doing wrong — he is always challenging me?" I can well remember myself saying to Karl on more than one occasion, "I am at my wits end — what am I going to do?"

We became mutual outlets for each other, a venting ground where we could air the many frustrations and concerns that we were constantly facing. This was also a time when we were able to provide each other insight into our children's past. This helped add perspective to what life was like before we arrived. Scores of understanding were written into our psyches when we began to understand the *reasons behind the behavior.* I would urge you, above all else, to keep the lines of communication open between you and your spouse. In light of the obstacles you will face each day, you owe it to each other and to your children.

Lastly, I would like to address the issue of sibling communication. You know, the ability to impart, to convey, to reveal, and to exchange feelings and information from one sibling to another. When we were first married, our children believed that this could best be done by arming and launching their deadliest verbal missiles.

The intent, of course, was to knock out the enemy. And believe me, they weren't just interested in stunning their victim; they were looking for total termination. When this didn't happen, I heard the name "*Mom*" screeched from one end of my house to another by some pretty seasoned vocal cords. I mediated more fights in those early days than a retired referee in the National Hockey League. It wasn't long before I came to the conclusion that it was time for these kiddos to begin to resolve their differences without my help. In my speech from the royal box, I asked each of them to make every effort to iron out their individual conflicts without parental interference. Even though I knew we would see more failures than successes in the beginning, I still believed that true bonding would never take place until they had learned to express their thoughts and feelings to each other in a constructive way.

At this point, I would like to offer a word of caution should you decide to heed my advice. Do not expect to always like or agree with the way in which they negotiate their peace talks. I have been reprimanded more than once for interfering in what they considered to be a fair and equitable union deal. "Mom," they said, "you told us to try and handle things between ourselves and now you're butting in." They were right, and I was wrong. Mother Hubbard, should have backed off!

There are times, however, when it is appropriate for you to don your black robe for needed arbitration. The prosecution and defense are definitely out of control, and it is time for the judge to get order in the courtroom. We had a few ground rules while our court was in session, and they were as follows:

- no one could interrupt during opening and closing arguments;
- they had the right to accuse, not annihilate;
- and all rhetoric had to be laced with kindness.

During those sessions, our children were given the freedom to present the problem from their angle as well as the responsibility to listen to the views of their opponent. Presented to the court were exhibits of anger, frustration, resentment, and tears. We were looking for middle ground, for those compromises that everyone could live with. These confrontations were growing experiences for each one of us. A perfect family we were not...we had lots of struggles. But the one thing we were learning to do was to communicate with each other. By the way, in time, these conflicts became the exception, not the rule. It has been my experience that even though emotional unleashing can be very painful, the after-shock can have a tremendous binding effect. Let me illustrate with a poignant story of both isolation and attachment.

Of all the relationships within our family which initially took the most lumps, it was the one between Rachel and Brian. Since he constantly got orders from his older sisters, he got a real "high" from bossing his two younger sisters around. Christy learned to ignore his demands while Rachel revolted at every turn. And I mean every turn. They were like oil and water. The more she resisted, the harder he was on her. She, in turn, quickly discovered many subtle ways of pushing his "Irritation" button.

I constantly asked the Lord to give them a deep love for each other. He was the only one who could bind together, with love, the pieces of this fractured fraternity. I must admit, though, that there were times when even I questioned the Lord's ability to change these two young people. And even though they had taken up permanent residency in my court (they filled most of my docket), their inner frustration with each other remained very focused.

One night, while I was in bed reading, the quietness of our home was interrupted by two screaming teenagers. You guessed it — Brian and Rachel. After calling them up to my room, we proceeded with the specifics of "he said, she said". The story went something like this. Rachel was reading a book in the kitchen. Brian had just finished watching television and on his way to bed asked Rachel, "What are you doing?" With all the sarcasm she could possibly muster, she replied, "I'm reading". Further pressing her, he asked, "Well, what are you reading?" "A book!" she snapped. Well, that was all he needed to hear. The accusations began, the prejudgments were announced, and a royal fight was under way. Or maybe I should say, I thought a World War had erupted.

Brian made it quite clear that he thought her comments were "snobby" and that it was high time for her to change her "uppity" attitude (his perception, of course). She wasn't at all interested in his opinion or his comments and promptly told him, "You don't know what you're talking about." As the proceedings continued, the tears began to roll, and I was afraid that this confrontation had the potential for some serious bruising. Their words were sharp and their jabs piercing.

Brian lectured her on the adverse affect her "superior and condescending" attitude would have on her friendships. Right in the midst of this hostile speech, his tone began to change. "I'm not saying that I have the most friends in the world," he said, "and I'm not saying that I'm always a good friend but…" He paused, looked right at her and said, "What I am saying is that I hate seeing you walk down the halls at school alone and I hate leaving the house to go out with my friends and know you're sitting home alone. It kills me." With that, he got up and left the room. (What Brian didn't know was that Rachel had been put in classes that contained mostly upperclassmen and she was finding it hard, because of her schedule, to be with friends her own age. This and other reasons, made friendships a struggle for her.)

By this time, she was sobbing. We sat in silence for a long time before I said, "Without coming out and saying the actual words, Rachel, he just told you that he loved you." This was a powerful moment for this brother and sister. A bond was established that night that totally changed the face of this relationship. The breakthrough came because of God and communication. You see, all along, without them even knowing, God had been bringing love into each of their hearts. He had been quietly doing His work in His time and in His way. That night, He used the vehicle of communication as the key to discover the changes He had made. It was a moment I will never forget since it was eight years in the making.

Chapter 4

Equality — An Absolute Must

*"I thank God that you are my mother.
You have made me into the person I am
today and I don't know what I'd do without your guidance, love and support."*

Rachel

One way to smooth the rough seas of blending is to be sure not to show partiality to one child over another. Let me issue a warning bulletin to the co-captains of the ship: Inequality or favoritism is the quickest way to disaster! This type of discrimination will breed an epidemic of resentment that will spread through your home like locusts upon a field.

It is important to remember the enormous adjustments that are placed upon the children of a blended family. Almost overnight, they are literally forced to share their custodial parent with virtual strangers. The mom or dad they once had all to themselves is now being billed on the home front as a common possession of two families. This is difficult stuff for a child who has become accustomed to being "top dog" in their single parent home.

The reality of this truth came alive to me during my first day in Karl's home. I was reading a book to Rachel and Christy when Rachel interrupted and asked me a question about the story. "Mom," she asked, "why did the little girl do that?" Before I could answer, Christy screamed, "She is not your mother! She is my mother!" By the way Rachel addressed me, it was clear that she was looking for a mother in her life and by the way Christy reacted, it was equally as clear that she had no interest in sharing the mother she already had. Even though I tried to convince these young gals that I wanted to be a mother to them both, it was going to take months of assurance for them to reconcile these overwhelming changes in their lives.

As you can see, there is a wide range of emotions awaiting entrance into the inner sanctum of a blended child. Even saying these adjustments are enormous is a gross understatement. With all this in mind now, I would like you to go one step further and imagine how even more difficult it would be for a child to realize that they were not one of their new parent's favorites. Try and feel the pain they would absorb when they became aware they were second choice in the family draft. Even as I write these words, my depth of conviction is strengthened in this area. No child should be exposed to this type of heartache. The biting pain of favoritism can literally cripple the overall well-being of a blended home.

From the day you enter their lives, each of your children will be watching you to see if you treat any of them differently. I learned quickly that I had a twenty-four-hour audience watching my every move, looking for any sign that told them that I treated one better than another. Complying with this expectation was not an easy task. Even as much as I may have wanted to deny it, I was aware of my tendency to favor my natural children during those early days. I tended to side with them should an argument arise; I tended to come down harder on my new children should a mishap occur; I tended to put up with more baloney from my natural children when the bull started to fly; I even saw myself having less sympathy for my new children when they were sick. Of course, this bothered me terribly. My sincere desire was to treat all my children on an equal basis.

I distinctly recall an occasion when my failure to deal equally forced me to make some instant decisions about my own attitude and behavior. Shortly after we were married, Rachel woke up one morning in tears, crying, "Mom, my ear hurts." Since it was quite early and it would be hours before the doctor's office opened, I rocked her for hours. There were times when she literally sobbed in pain. At one point, I became so exasperated with her crying that I sharply told her to "toughen up". Can you imagine my telling a six-year-old to stop crying when her ear was throbbing in pain. I was so ashamed of myself. My own partiality had shown through. After receiving a self-inflicted scolding, I made an early morning pledge which promoted the ideal that this young gal *deserved* the same love and concern that I would have offered my biological children and *nothing less.*

Equality is an easy word to say but quite another to act out. I was constantly challenged to "strike a balance" among our troops at all times for they were quick to use such accusations as "That's not fair!" or "You didn't treat him that way." Sometimes their indictments of me were very undeserved but there were other times when their call was right on the mark. (I could tell by the invisible tomatoes being thrown in my direction!) I had shown favoritism.

Because of the different age groups within our family, we constantly struggled with the boundaries and privileges of a first grader versus a teenager. This whole area proved to be a mine field for both Karl and me. We never knew where the explosion of "that's not fair" would come from next. The younger children used such complaints as "It's not fair that the older ones get to stay up longer," while the teenagers' protests included "It isn't fair that we have to pick up the kitchen again while they get to go out and play." These verbal demonstrations were non-ending and especially wearing on us as parents of a large, blended family. We learned to make individual calls according to individual situations and made it clear to the peanut gallery that "nothing in life is fair". This old adage was used many times during those early months as we tried to show our children that in the end, everything would balance itself out. This meant that sometimes we would do things their way, sometimes we would do things their brother's way, sometimes we would do things their sister's way, and sometimes we would do things our way. It was by using a formula of good judgment and common sense that we were taken a long way on our passage toward "Unity Junction".

Acquiring a taste for equality must be a priority for both parents, and committing this habit to memory must be a part of all interactions. Please do not let my brutal honesty discourage you, though. I have opted to give you the real life picture of both the positive intentions and the negative tendencies you will experience on the first leg of your race toward blending. But once the dynamic of bonding begins to take place, your sense of equality becomes second nature. In fact, I personally buried this issue a long time ago.

On a lighter note, the price tag for "equality" in our home became one costly venture. Remember, we blended five children. This meant that when one asked for an ice cream at the mall, the other four would want one as well. And when one of them asked to bring a friend home after church, the others would automatically make the same request. There were Sundays when I unexpectedly had twelve people for dinner! (The longer we were together, the easier it was for us to introduce the concept of "taking turns".) This also came to mean that when one of my girls asked me to give her a perm, there would be three others waiting in the wings. One Easter, I literally rolled hair for six hours. Our house smelled like a chemical factory in full production. And my husband quickly learned during our ski trips to New Hampshire that a single request for something from the snack bar really meant five hot chocolates, five french fries, and five M&M's!

My favorite story of all was the time when all four of our girls took dancing lessons. Now for those of you who are not familiar with the dance culture, this meant I had to buy four pairs of ballet shoes, four pairs of tap shoes and four sets of leotards, not to mention the cost of the individual lessons each week. Katy and Amy took tap, ballet, and jazz, while Rachel and Christy took tap and ballet. Their lessons ran every Friday from 3:00-6:30 p.m.

I thought this was rough until they announced the program for the upcoming recital. Since all of them were in different routines, we were required to buy 10 costumes at $25 a piece, and we also had to pay $7 a ticket for each of our family and friends. To top it all off, the temperature on the day of the recital was 97 degrees, and we had to sit in a non-air-conditioned auditorium for 4½ hours (it was a death sentence)! My brother, Bob, who lived with us at the time, sat through the entire performance and to this day, constantly reminds the girls of his tremendous sacrifice on their behalf!

When it came to Halloween, I felt just like the Fairy Godmother in Cinderella as I tried to use my magic on all five costumes for the big night. I searched the nooks and crannies of our house for any odds and ends that might fit the bill. If I couldn't find it on the home front, I scouted the local stores. Over the years, we have collected quite an assortment of characters, such as, Raggedy Ann, Cleopatra, Happy the Clown, G.I. Joe, Scarlett O'Hara and the Great Pumpkin, to name a few. As our children walked through the door each year for neighborhood trick or treat, their path was lit by five large pumpkins which had been carved on my kitchen floor a week earlier (there were seeds everywhere)! Five was always the magic number in our house!

The greatest challenge of all though was Christmas. A few months before December 25, I asked each of my children to come up with their own "Wish List" so I would have lots of options from which to pick when I hit the marketplace. After only a few weeks of shopping, I found it necessary to hide these multiple finds from one end of the house to the other. I quickly came to the conclusion that if I was ever going to find these gifts again, I was going to have to master the art of record keeping. Since I was buying so many gifts (friends and family as well), organization had to be the buzz word of my existence.

In order to complete my mission, I developed a master list for gifts bought, gifts needed, and gifts distributed. You see, my husband's Swedish tradition calls for the opening of all gifts on Christmas Eve while my family had always opened theirs on Christmas Day. As a compromise, we decided to let the children open half at night and half in the morning. In order for all of this to take place, all gifts had to be coded "AM" or "PM" on both the tags and my master list and coded by number in case there was a mix-up. To further complicate matters, PM gifts could only be put under the living room tree while AM gifts belonged under the family room tree. Also, we were careful to purchase an equal number of gifts for each of our children.

This was an incredible process. My friends would always shake their heads in disbelief when they saw the number of lists tucked away in my pocketbook. The reason we went to all this effort was to reinforce, once again, their individual value within our home. We wanted to strengthen their belief in our desire to show equality to each of our children. Equality in this case really meant exhaustion for one tired Mom and Dad. But it was worth it. It is these specialized details that helps bind families...that "extra mile" that makes all the difference.

It is at this point that I will go to the top of my lighthouse, shine my beacon, and sound my foghorn with the following warning: *Do not* refer to your spouse's children as your stepchildren. There is nothing that leads to parental and sibling polarization more than the use of the word "step". I am convinced that the type of relationship I now enjoy with my new children would have never taken place if they had been constantly categorized as my "stepchildren". The words of Florence Pauls (from Chapter 2) bear repeating in light of this whole subject, "When you marry that guy or gal, you marry that person's children, too — you really do. You'd better think it through before you take it on." In other words, your spouse's children, by virtue of the vows you made, become your children as well. This is not a matter of first and second class children. They do not need to be reminded on a daily basis of how they got to be your children. They are now yours. You are responsible for meeting their emotional and physical needs. The label "stepchild" just doesn't fit.

To this day, I cringe whenever I hear someone introduce their child to me in this way. The rude part of my personality is tempted to ask if that really means that this child is not quite as important as their biological child? Can you imagine being a five-year-old little girl and having to hear your new mother introduce you and your new sister as, "This is my daughter, Suzie and this is my stepdaughter, Donna." It almost seems like a form of bigotry.

My children, in an honest discussion with me years ago, shared the reasons why they resented being called stepchildren. First of all, since we were working hard to build a new identity, they felt these words were a throwback to the days of "yours" and "mine", definitely not to "ours". Second, the word "step" symbolized to them the feeling of being on the outside looking in. It meant second-best, second-rate, and second-hand. Because of these reasons, Karl and I made a conscious decision never to refer to each other's children as "step-anything". If they chose to call us stepmother or step-father, that was their decision. Ironically though, since they never heard us call them "stepchildren", we were never referred to as "stepparents".

The insensitivity of others in this area is appalling to us, even after being together for twelve years. We continue to have people introduce our children as "Karl's daughter" or "Sharon's son" instead of "Karl's and Sharon's son or daughter". Our children are hurt whenever such callousness as this is displayed. My husband and I have come to the point where we correct those who seem to feel the need of making this distinction about our family. I would encourage you to do the same.

I appreciated a comment recently made by a new friend after hearing the outline of this book. She turned to me and said, "Sharon, whose children are whose...I don't even know." Before I could respond, she added, "No, don't tell me; it really doesn't matter, does it?" She had grasped the reality of what we had come to believe, "it really doesn't matter...they are all 'ours'!"

Let me share with you a story about how one of our children responded to this type of segregation. One day, a new acquaintance was visiting our home and was especially interested in our family pictures on the stairwell. She turned to me in front of the children and said, "Who belongs to whom?" I felt uncomfortable with the entire situation but answered her question quickly and moved on to other issues. When she left, my oldest daughter, who was visibly upset, took me aside and said, "Mom, the next time that question is ever asked of you, do not answer it. It doesn't make any difference whose was whose...we are a family now. That is all that matters." Since that time, whenever I am asked that question, my answer always is, "I don't remember!"

Chapter 5

Discipline — Tricky Ground

> *"It hasn't been until lately that I've begun to understand the reasons behind a lot of the things you have done to me — for my own good. Thanks for not taking the easy way out."*
>
> Katy

"I am not eating this supper and you can't make me," said this half-pint, spitfire during our first week of marriage. Rachel's fearless challenge told me the honeymoon was now over. Her words were used as bait to see how far she could go with me and how much I would really take. After taking a deep breath, I announced the following: "Young lady, you will eat everything on that plate and you will sit here until it is done. Is that clear?" This was to be a war of wills and for a six-year-old, she was no slouch! She had no intention of giving in and literally sat at the table for hours. In fact, she fell asleep while on her food watch!

This was to be one of hundreds of confrontations that Karl and I would face during those early years. My journal had this to say about Rachel after only six months of marriage, *"I feel I have come a long way with her but she can truly be a 'tester' when she has the urge, and I have had to come down pretty hard on her at times."* Just think, she was just one of five!

As in every large family, we had a variety of personalities. Some were more passive, some more aggressive, and some were a little bit of both. Our two oldest daughters, Katy and Amy, did little in the way of testing the boundaries before them. They are especially sensitive girls and the trauma of divorce within their own family had left many scars. They were looking for peace and security, and because of this and their own coopera- tive natures, we had few struggles with them in the area of discipline. As a matter of fact, if parenthood consisted of raising children like these girls, I would have classified it as being one of the easiest jobs imaginable. I would have never been able to relate with those of my peers who were living with children that inspired books such as, The Strong Willed Child, By Dr. Dobson.

God gave us one such child to keep us humble. His name is Brian. At the time of our blending, he was the only boy, the middle child and a reincarnation of Patrick Henry. His motto was, "Give me liberty or give me death". A section of my journal relates these find- ings, *"Brian's will is stronger than anyone's in our family, and it is difficult to have the consistency in disciplining that we must have."* From the very begin- ning, he and Karl locked horns often and, to this day, they can reenact with accuracy "Custer's Last Stand"! Again, my journal reported the following, *"Brian and Karl certainly had a showdown today. Karl was the firmest he has ever been. Brian loves to challenge him and takes every opportunity to gain authority. Karl really should be tougher.* "

Lastly, our cast of players included our younger daughters, Rachel and Christy. They, too, possessed sensitive natures similar to their female siblings, but they tended to be a bit more fiery in spirit. They were more eager to explore the limits of their verbal and physical behavior. Our gang was certainly a challenge!

The reason I used the words "tricky ground" in the title of this chapter stems from the fact that single parents have a tendency to go easy on their children. When you, their new parent, arrive with your own pack of rules and expectations, there is bound to be resistance and opposition to your new leadership. When this happens (and this will happen), the floor beneath you will seem a bit slippery as you begin to confront the infractions to your new set of standards. Even though you are aware that your children will, at one time or another, defy the rules before them, it is important for you to understand that you will have a tendency to receive these frontal attacks better from your natural children than you will from your new children.

In order to cope with this strain, I immediately became the world's best tattletale. By this I mean that I reported all my new children's misbehavior to their father as soon as he came through the door. After all, I didn't want my new children to hate me or to tell their friends that I reminded them of the wicked stepmother in Cinderella, so I tiptoed around this whole area of discipline. If this weren't bad enough, I also found myself coming down harder on my natural children than ever before. Not that their behavior was any worse than the others, but

I took my frustration out on them because there was a sense of comfort and familiarity that I didn't yet feel with Karl's children.

Even though initially, I believe, it is easier on the children when discipline comes from the natural parent, it must also be established that the new parent, by virtue of their role in the home, has the authority to discipline rebellious offspring. Not only do I think the new parent has the authority, I believe they have an obligation to their spouse, to the children and to the formation of a healthy home. It wasn't fair of me to make Karl the "heavy" when insurrections came from our masses. Our home didn't need a mealy-mouthed maid, but it did need a take-charge mother.

In order for these relationships to flourish, your new child needs to be allowed the freedom to test you. They need to measure the dimensions of the support systems you are offering, and they also need to know that at the first point of conflict, you are not on your way out the door. All these challenging emotions are a normal part of the blending process between a new parent and the child.

Even though I have used the word authority, please do not make the assumption that this means automatic respect. Respect, within a blended home, must be both demanded (outward respect) and earned (inner respect). Let me illustrate. During one of my recent seminars, a lady in the audience raised her hand and asked me about the issue of respect within our home. She went on to give a brief explanation of how her new children didn't respect her at all. Their comments were consistently mean and their behavior was atrocious. She started to cry as she unfolded a tale of how the natural mother promoted this type of behavior while the children were on visitation outings. This lady was in deep pain because she had *allowed* the basic courtesy of respect to go unused in her new home. She should have made it very clear from day one that she *expected* from their words and actions a strong degree of respect. The type of behavior she was living with was totally unacceptable, and it should have never been tolerated.

A new parent should be treated with the same respect that the new child would show a soccer coach, a school teacher or a friend's mother. I would encourage you, as a new parent, to accept nothing less. Do not allow yourself to be demeaned by your new child. Demand their outward respect.

Inner respect, though, must be earned and will take time to develop. A sense of inner esteem will only begin to grow after your children become convinced of your desire to meet their needs. Five years ago, Katy sent me a card on my birthday with this message, "It hasn't been until lately that I have begun to understand the reasons behind a lot of the things you have done to me, for my own good. Thanks for not taking the easy way out." You see, it was *time* that allowed her to take ownership of the fact that I really did have her best interest at heart and, again, it was *time* that made her begin to appreciate the fact that "confronting really meant caring". The type of overseeing about which I have been speaking is responsible for pushing your new child out of the valley in which they had settled and on toward a higher mountain.

To this day, I continue to tell my children how thankful they should be that "I am on their case", because by doing so, I am really showing them how much I love them and how much I care about who they become. I knew my seven-year-old son must have been listening to me (at least this once) when he got in the car one day and said, "Mom, you see that boy over there, I don't think his mother loves him, because whenever he does something wrong, he never gets in trouble." Will your children test you? Certainly. Are you expected to be a doormat for children in transition? Absolutely not. As much as they may resist, I believe they are secretly hoping that you use the weight you carry. Remember, according to experts, young people find security in loving discipline.

Another area of adjustment for blended parents is the tremendous sensitivity they feel when their natural child is scolded or punished by their new parent. This can be one painful issue in those early years. The tendency to be thin-skinned and touchy in this area is caused by their "parental protection reflex" (PPR). Single parents, for the most part, have just spent the past 2+ years shielding their child from anymore pain (this can be from either death or divorce). Having to listen to the rebukes of an "outsider" (at least in the beginning) can hit the rawest of nerves.

I have been especially honest with you throughout this book, so I will continue by saying that this was a very difficult area (and I mean difficult) for me as a mother. There were times when my heart stood still as I witnessed the chastisement of one of my children by my new husband, even when I knew it was deserved. That

PPR is a powerful emotion. You will never be able to erase it, but you will be able to share it, in time. It has been my experience that the more I observed the love and concern my spouse had for my children, the more I began to appreciate his backing and encouragement in the rearing of my precious children. The same was true of Karl.

I must admit though that there are still times when my innate sense of guardianship is awakened by a cross look or an undeserved verbal lashing. *It is at these times especially that you will be tempted to intervene on behalf of your child. Please do not do this in front of your children. Speak only of your objections to your spouse when you are alone! It is vitally important that you support your spouse, in the area of discipline in front of your children.*

There have been incidents, for example, when I totally disagreed with the way my husband handled my son. Internally, I sided with Brian because I didn't feel he deserved the response he had received, but externally, my reaction never displayed my inner discontent with Karl's behavior. This scenario was played, at one time or another, with each of our children during the past twelve years. We experienced controversy over the individual disciplinary actions of each other. Most parents do from time to time. It became the custom to pull each other aside and immediately express our feelings. These clashes took place in the privacy of our room, our car, or during a walk, but never in front of the children. Our exchanges were considered classified and deemed top secret from our children.

I have observed homes in which parents have sided with their natural children instead of their spouse in the midst of a family conflict. The result was chaos. These children began to play one parent against the other and the strain on the marriage began to show some serious cracking. The children used the art of manipulation to their advantage and eventually were successful in widening the growing rift between their parents. Do not allow your children to tinker in this type of double dealing. By all means, share the feelings of misgiving you have with your spouse but above all else, stay united in front of your children.

This has been an especially difficult chapter for me to write, because whenever I thought of the word discipline, I automatically thought of the name Brian. He was always in trouble in our home. It was so frustrating for both Karl and me since all the punishment in the world did not seem to alter his attitude or behavior. I continued to get defensive with Karl's handling of Brian and Karl, in turn, remained perplexed as to how to alter this cycle of verbal engagement.

In spite of this, though, I knew that if I had outwardly sided with Brian during those confrontations, we would have faced some serious problems down the road, especially during those teenage years. Karl and I tried, the best we knew how, to stand united on the home front. I cannot even put into words the piercing pain I often felt at these never ending conflicts. It wasn't until seventh grade that Brian was diagnosed with the syndrome, "Attention Deficit Disorder", and we learned for the first time of his inability to control his own behavior. The world was in constant motion for this young man and sadly enough, until this point, we believed that the more his will was broken, the more control he would have over his behavior. We had been wrong for a very long time. In fact, the doctor who did his testing in Boston, told us that she was amazed his self-esteem was as intact as it was, in light of the fact that he had been reprimanded constantly for twelve years.

I have shared this story with you because each blended family will have children in their midst who will be easier to deal with than others. There is no such thing as a perfect family, let alone a perfect blended family. All families have difficulties. Even though we are all aware of this fact, we are still secretly hoping that the setting of our home reflects the fairy-tale notion that children will do whatever they are told. We are not interested in dealing with the hassles of which I have spoken, rather, we are looking for problem-free living. It simply does not exist. Struggles within a blended family are part of everyday life and are an inevitable part of the whole process.

In light of this, be especially sensitive to each of your children in this whole area of discipline, and always seek to understand the reasons behind the behavior. We have made mistakes, as I'm sure you will, too, but try and keep foremost in your mind the best interest of your child, whenever you see the need to discipline.

During Brian's early teen years, the phrase "you are grounded" became a familiar phrase around our house. On one such occasion, he left the house without permission while we were out for dinner. He wrote the following note and left it on our bed:

Mom & Dad,

As you know, I've been going through some pretty hard times lately. I know everybody has hard times but I honestly can't handle them right now. I know you are upset with me right now because I'm not at home and, Mom, please don't cry. Don't be mad at me, please. I hate when you're mad at me. I'm hurting really bad inside and I need to be alone and talk to God. I really need his guidance right now. Please do not be upset with me. I love you very, very much. I'll be home tomorrow. Please don't be mad.

Love,
Brian

That was a long night for Karl and me. We had no idea where he was. So many thoughts raced through our heads. What had we done wrong? What could we do to help? When he returned home the next day, we had a long talk with this hurting teenager. A lot of sharing was done in our backyard that afternoon. Some strides were made, some reassurances were offered, and some healing took place.

There are times when discipline is in order, but this was not one of those times. We, as parents, were being called to reach out and understand the struggles of our adolescent son. And since you, no doubt, will be confronted with similar situations in the years to come, may God grant you the wisdom to know when to punish and when to pardon.

Chapter 6

Bonding Takes Time

> *"This year has been a tough one on our relationship but I think we're coming out of it and possess, hopefully, an even stronger one than before because of it."*
>
> Katy

"Each child is a joy to me and so special in many different ways," cited my journal after our first year together. Those twelve months had been the longest I had ever known, but I was always praising God for this new beginning, even with all its challenges! I rapidly discovered that each one of my children would handle this adjustment differently and for unique reasons. The oldest from each family had an especially difficult time. Katy, age 13, felt I was a real threat and Brian, age 7, was disgusted with the whole idea of being the only boy and having four sisters!

Katy and Brian clashed often and in full mouth to mouth combat! She was eager to establish age superiority and often pulled rank when it came to the way things should be done or even in the way they played. He, on the other hand, had no intention of listening (or obeying) any of her orders and promptly told her at least one thousand times during those beginning months, "You are not my mother."

These were difficult days for this little boy. Not only was he having to cope with his new position as middle child, he was also contending with the rough and tumble world of a new family, a new school, and new friends. These inner struggles manifested themselves immediately. He became a fresh, mouthy, stubborn, and angry camper who constantly challenged us on everything.

Katy's internal battles were played out by becoming critical, bored, and depressed all at the same time. She was having a hard enough time dealing with the mood swings of a teenager without having to open the door of her life to three intruders who were looking for "relative" status. There were times when she seemed very close and at others, very far away. An especially stinging issue for her was the matter of calling me "Mom". During one of our first tearful encounters, she told me that she felt I wanted her to accept me as her mother (like her sisters had done), but right now, she just couldn't. This was a point of real conflict for her and it would take months of bridge-building for us to experience the special closeness of mother and daughter.

Just as a box of candies has a wide assortment so did our "melting pot". Notes from my journal revealed that Amy, age 11, "*seemed so relaxed and was constantly trying to please me*"; Rachel, age 6, "*loved my attention...always wanted to kiss, hug, sit on my lap*" and Christy, age 5, "*was delighted with her new family.*"

Their positive attitudes brought tremendous encouragement when the going got tough.

It is important to remember these appraisals reflected attitudes that were displayed during our early months together. A healthy, blended family will continue to experience a metamorphosis of change for years to come. For example, even though Rachel "*loved my attention*" on one page of my journal, two months later, I reported that "*she wasn't satisfied with the attention I was giving her. She wanted more. Even though I felt she was happy with us, she definitely needed time to gain security in our situation.*"

The same was true of Katy. The reflections within my journal paint with clarity the variety of mood swings we were feeling within our relationships. During the first month, I wrote this stark commentary, "*We definitely have a wall between us.*" After three months, I sketched a brighter outlook with these words, "*There are times when I feel she really tries to make an effort to be close.*" The script would change, once again, after six months when I revealed, "*We definitely have a long way to go. I'm trying hard to understand her.*" Yet another tone shift occurred after nine months as found in this inscription, "*She seems more relaxed and we seem to be closer these days.*" And finally, as we rounded the corner on that first year, I penned, "*She and I certainly have come a long way. I believe she resented my presence and authority here at first, but things seem to be evening themselves out.*" After some long, dark days, we were beginning to see some sunlight.

These intimate scribbles of our own struggles make good my assertion that the art of blending is not learned in a single day, during a full week, or even through an entire year. It is a pilgrimage of sorts and its members are, as Webster so aptly puts it, "pilgrims — strangers in a foreign land". We were basically strangers when our families married. We had no idea where the road before us would lead. What we did know was that we had made a commitment to each other and our children, and on that basis alone, we proceeded with life in the blended lane. Our journey included both the routine rituals and the special events of everyday life. Our itinerary involved the inescapable twists and turns of normal living.

A true alliance can only take place between these strangers as they learn to face the highs and lows of life together. It is the laughter and tears and the disappointments and triumphs that actually pump life into a new family. Consequently, the type of bonding to which I have been referring can only happen with *time*. It takes time for these individuals to begin to feel comfortable and at home in their new surroundings. In fact, as I look back over the past twelve years, *I now realize time was my friend.* You see, the longer we were together, the stronger the ties between us became. Reminding yourself of this vital truth can provide a resurgence of hope when you are knee deep in domestic havoc. The quest for approval among the members of a blended family takes years to resolve.

The journey you are on will include opposition, antagonism, polarity, clashing, resistance, interference, and friction. You will experience each of these emotions at one time or another in your new home. There will be roadblocks, detours, and setbacks. There will be times when you will feel that you have taken three steps forward and two steps backward. On your worst of days, you will even want to quit and give up. You will rationalize that perhaps this was a mistake from the beginning and there is no way that you will all come together as a family. Quite frankly, there will be moments when you are not even sure that you like your new children and you are equally sure they do not like you. Often you will feel unwanted, unloved, and unappreciated. In spite of all of this, though, I would encourage and urge you to press on, hold on, run on, and carry on or, in other words, persevere. E.B. Michaels once said, "Perseverance is the investment, success is the return."

Give these relationships the time they deserve. They don't come together overnight but they do offer such wonderful possibilities. How do I know? Listen to the words written on my birthday card from Katy four years ago, "Mom, I have no idea how you do what you do. You certainly are an inspiration to me. I don't always tell you how much I appreciate you for who you are and what you do for me but I want you to know that I do. God sure knew what He was doing when He gave me you". I have received similar cards from all my children. They are considered some of my most priceless treasures.

I must repeat once again that blending families is a process, not a one time event. Follow my own evaluations of our family during our first year together and notice the strides we made. *"The kids are beginning to show more warmth and tolerance for each other which certainly helps me"..."I believe we have made progress over the past few months as far as closeness goes; in fact,*

*the kids follow me from room to room"..."it amazes me
how the months have passed so quickly; at times, I feel we
have come so far and at others, the journey seems, oh, so
long."*

You see, the struggle and drudgery of authentic
bonding can never be played out to a set time schedule.
Each family will move at its own pace, depending on the
efforts of the parents and children. In light of this, it is
imperative that you allow each of your children "liberty
of passage" through the maze of emotions necessary to
establish a love connection. The teenagers would say
each of them "needs room". Allow them space to adjust
to the enormous changes in their lives. Many of these
children need to walk through the valley of resentment
and hostility before they can reach the peak of acceptance
and gratitude. Trying to repress these inner struggles will
only add to the tension in your home.

As previously mentioned, communication must
play a large part in the passage through these various
emotions. Children need to be given the freedom of
expressing both their feelings of satisfaction and their
bristles of bitterness. Granting them liberty of passage is
a vital part of successful blending because each child will
respond differently to your situation. When you are able
to appreciate and accept their diversity, you will be able
to redefine your noble expectations for instant harmony.

Try not to favor the child who has embraced your
new family with open arms over the one who appears
distant and totally resistant to the whole idea of mixing
families. It is my belief that with love and a great deal of
prayer, these "slow pokes" will eventually be assimilated
into your new home, and sometimes in a far deeper way

than you could have ever imagined. Until that time, hold on to these hold-outs!

If you have asked God to give that child a deep love for their new parent and siblings, believe that He is in the process of doing just that. Once again, it will be done in His time and in His way. There will come a day, I assure you, when you will witness the sweet hand of God's spirit in these relationships. The special closeness you were longing to achieve is no longer a dream, but a wonderful reality.

As I was looking through our photo albums recently, I recalled with pleasure the many special times we have enjoyed as a family. None were more significant than the other but each event certainly brought us closer together. The summers we spent on Cape Cod (a summer resort on the East Coast) continue to be wonderful memories for each of us. Those carefree days when we hung together on the beach or challenged each other for hours in board games are recalled often in our home. During the winters, we enjoyed skiing with friends on some of New Hampshire's most beautiful mountains. A real camaraderie was established on those slopes each year. These were "binding moments" for our new family.

One of my early jottings was entitled, "Life and All Its Challenges" and in it I wrote, *"Many things have changed since my first days here in Boston...the kids seem to be doing better although we all have our days. There is such competition for 'rights' and 'affection'."* I don't know how I ever got through those constant arguments over personal rights and demanded affection. If I heard the phrase, "I'm first" once during those early days, I heard it one million times. They fought over such things as whose "right it was to sit in the front seat with me" or whose "right it was for first shower when we returned from the beach". As for affection, the younger ones fought over who was going to sit next to Mom at the restaurant or who got to hold my hand while walking through the mall. I was constantly challenged to please my masses at every turn. These conflicts were endless and extremely exhausting for us as parents.

Fortunately for us, each of our children was born with a wonderful sense of humor. Our funny bones were often tickled when we received cards that read, "Keep smiling, Mom, after all I could have been twins," or "Dad, according to recent statistics, it costs around $125,000 to raise a kid these days but that's a small price to pay for all the happiness we've brought you. Right, Dad?...I said, Right, Dad?" And even though our son, Brian (nicknamed "The Challenger") has the ability to change my hair color from a soft brown to a stark white in a matter of seconds, he can equally bring a spontaneous smile to my face with his wonderfully dry sense of humor. This birthday card from him is one my favorites, "Mom, you have the wisdom of the ages...the patience of a saint...the radar of a stealth bomber!"

Their letters from summer camp were hysterical. Here is a sampling of some from our three younger children. Christy wrote, "I miss you a lot. I twisted my thumb. A girl solted (translation: stole) my money. I am having fun. Goodbye." Rachel's even more colorful letter included, "Well, camp was good until this morning. I threw up." And Brian's note was short, sweet and right to the point with "Hi. How are you? I'm fine. Camp is great. Please send me a care package with the following: Nestle Quik juice boxes, Fruity Pebbles and *money*. I'm really running short!"

They were equally as humorous with each other. Brian thought nothing of sending his younger sister this card on her first teenage birthday, "Now that you're 13, I guess you're no longer a *twerp*...so Happy Birthday, *punk*!" And Amy joined in with this gushy card, "To my sister on her birthday...whenever I think back of the way I treated you when we were young, the mindless jokes, the cruel taunts...it cheers me right up."

Even though our children have the ability to be quick-witted, I think we would all agree that our home was blessed with a resident clown. Christy was known for the constant butchering of the English language and her inevitable tendency to be a total klutz. We have enjoyed many laughs over her comical antics. I thank God our children are so lighthearted. These moments gave us the ability not to take our present situation too seriously. Please accept this piece of practical advice: If you don't have a sense of humor, run out and get one. You are going to need it. Looking for humor in everyday situations will definitely keep you sane.

Every once in a while, when I became totally discouraged with our progress, a ray of hope would emerge from within our own evolving family. I clearly remember such an incident when some of our children were away on an extended visitation. The day before they were to arrive home, their siblings took it upon themselves to paint a large banner across our barn door with the words, "Welcome Home". This message was simple enough for those driving by our house, but no one knew, like my husband and I did, the true significance of those words. We were finally beginning to experience the true meaning of the word, bonding. Indeed, we were on our way to becoming a family unit.

I also found that often, when I was drowning in a sea of frustration and unfulfillment, the Lord would send me a lifesaver of encouragement (just in the nick of time)! One such time occurred when my neighbor shared with me one afternoon that "she had seen a real softness in attitude and a sense of appreciation in Katy toward me". Those simple words lightened my spirit and brought hope to my weary heart. My journal recorded quite often these words, *attitudes seem to be better...we seem to be getting closer.* " Remember, according to the experts and my own personal experience, it takes 2-5 years for a blended family to begin to emerge.

I believe with all my heart that prayer was the major factor which brought wholeness to our family life. I will end this book with it's tremendous impact on our lives. Don't underestimate the power of prayer. These words of appreciation from Brian and Katy provide hope for all blended families as they learn to stand the test of time.

> *"Mom, I hope you have seen a difference in my behavior because I am trying. Thank you for always being there when I need you. I love you very much. "*
> *Brian*

"On Valentine's, you tell people how much you love them. I love you very much — your my best friend and I want to thank you for all your time, effort and love. I'm proud to call you mother...you are very special to me."

Katy

Chapter 7

Expect Criticism

*Lord, help me to remember that nothing is
going to happen to me today that you and
I can't handle together.*

The dreamer within me truly believed our life as
a blended family would look just like the popular TV
series, *"The Brady Bunch."* I envisioned life being as
smooth and predictable as *"Father Knows Best"* and
"Leave It To Beaver." And I also believed that "my
responses to daily domestic crises would be controlled
with just the right amount of peaceful negotiations and
quoted Scripture...my husband would stand in awesome
respect whenever I entered the room...my children would
have bumper stickers on the back of their bikes that read,
'Have you hugged your mother today?'," as Joyce
Landorf Heatherley puts it in her book, Changepoints.

None of these visionary expectations became
concrete truth in my life. As a matter of fact, I wrote
this honest response in my journal as to what life was like

in the blended lane at one point. *"Today has been one of those hard days when the whole responsibility seems too much and I would like to get up and walk away from it all (or at least for a week's vacation)."* Mike and Carol Brady were reading lines from a script...we were dealing with the science of reality. And part of that reality would include criticism from my new children, from our extended families, and from the outside world as well.

I must have been incredibly naive when I married Karl because it never occurred to me that when I entered his home, I would be in constant competition with a "mother" who already lived there. "Who was she?" you ask. Her name was Katy and she was thirteen years old. She was a tad young to be a mother but, because of the responsibilities heaped upon her as the oldest child of divorced parents, she had been forced to become a miniature matriarch.

You see, many times, when children have been functioning in a home without one parent, they begin to compensate for the slack. The young girl becomes the mother — the young boy, the father. They play out these roles as effectively as possible and come to believe their mode of operation to be superior. This can become a constant rub as domestic and child-rearing responsibilities are transferred from the child to the new parent. This was especially true of Katy. Now you can understand her resistance to my presence. It was a good thing I was so determined to make this marriage work, because I was dealing with one strong young lady.

Even now as I look back upon a number of incidents that triggered a response of resentment toward me, I am convinced there was no possible way of our avoiding these nose-to-nose confrontations. After all, the structure of her home had changed, and she was no longer second in command. And even though I understood where she was coming from and had great sympathy for the enormous pain she had undergone, I could not allow her to take control. Did she receive this mandate with a standing ovation? Absolutely not, but it was imperative the officer on deck take command. Criticism then became the defense mechanism for this former dictator (at least to her younger sisters). Let me give you an example.

One afternoon while the kids were outside playing, an argument arose over a particular toy. Katy, who had been watching everything through the window, immediately decided to take matters into her own hands. After bolting out our front door, she promptly reprimanded the one whom she believed to be the guilty party. As usual, the target was Brian. By the time I heard the multiple screams and had arrived on the scene, she not only had verbally scolded her younger brother but had also given him one solid whack. A gutsy surge of power on her part to be sure. After establishing a peace treaty between the younger children, I came into the house for a heart to heart talk with my eldest daughter. This incident had set in motion a much needed confrontation over her constant interference in what I believed to be my parenting duties. Up to this point I had tried to display great patience in this whole area, but this time she had gone too far.

As we talked, I tried to make it crystal clear to her that it was my responsibility, not hers, to correct and reprimand the children in our home. She had been relieved of duty the day I entered that house. I let her know in no uncertain terms that she was off base, and she needed to come to grips with these absolutes. This was not a negotiable issue. After hearing all I had to say, she looked at me and with chilling frankness said, "Well, you're not doing a very good job at it." This was no shrinking violet!

If that wasn't enough, her attempted coup during our first Christmas together, told me the battle was far from over. While the kids were at school one day, I unpacked all of our Christmas decorations and spent the entire day arranging candles, ribbons and figurines. Remember, we had two sets of everything so this was no small task. It took hours to unpack and garnish our large home with the hoards of knickknacks we had both accumulated.

Right before the school bus arrived, I left the house to take care of some banking for my husband. When I arrived home, I quickly discovered that someone had changed the entire Christmas scenery. Simply put, all the decorations had been rearranged! I had a real good idea who the culprit was so immediately went to confront the "other mother". "Why did you change everything?" I asked her with as much reserve as I could possibly muster. Without so much as a pause, she answered, "I didn't like the way you did it...I thought I could do a better job!" As I stood there stunned by her outright aggression, the light before my eyes turned a feverish red. You see, she was informing me in a rather blatant fashion that she wasn't at all interested in relinquishing her duties. After taking a deep breath, the following edict was declared in short order: "I'm the adult here...I am not your peer...I will do my best to meet your needs and make you happy and there will be times when you will be included in the decision-making process...but don't ever do anything like this again unless you've checked with me first...remember, I'm the boss here." Her exit that day reminded me of the Mad-Hatter in Alice in Wonderland.

You see, this confrontation was crucial in order for this young lady to be ultimately freed to begin to feel and act like an adolescent and not the "make shift" adult she had become. Even though life's circumstances had thrust her into this adult role, my journal shows her inner vulnerability when I wrote, "*She can be very independent and then a moment later, can draw back as a child needing help.*" Handing over the cloak of motherhood to me was very difficult for this young lady and was done so with deep resistance. Embarking on a new life with a new parent, for some children, is truly tough stuff. I know it was for Katy. Some resist these changes silently, while others resist with slanderous lampoons. It takes time for these children to trust you as a parent and allow you passage into their fragile world.

Not only did I have to accept criticism from my new children, I also had to deal with the occasional reproaches brought against me by my new extended family. This was an area for which I was totally unprepared as a new wife and mother. Even though I knew there were some within our family who had deep reservations about our marriage, I naively believed that once our union took place, these same people would shelve their concerns and play a large part in our support systems. What I didn't realize was that they were still reeling from the pain and separation of the initial divorce and what I didn't understand was how much more difficult it was going to be for them to embrace the complications introduced by our blended family.

I needed to be reminded, as will you, that life has changed for these people and in a big way. The family they once knew would never again be the same. The traditions they once shared would now be history. I quickly learned that some family members would accept these changes with buoyant resiliency while others would resist with stubborn antagonism.

What makes these situations so difficult is that the blended family is not just dealing with two sets of grand-parents and a few aunts and uncles. Quite often, there are four sets of grandparents and innumerable relatives from both sides and *each has their own set of expectations of this new family*. It is when these expectations are not met that the criticism begins (and the fur flies). It is during those early years of blending that the caretakers of a blended family can feel trounced upon by the continual verbal judgments of their peripheral family. I remember one such shot fired my way during my first year in Boston. Unintentionally, I didn't send one of the children's grandparents a Valentine's Day card. The following week I received a call telling me how hurt the person was by my oversight. Unbeknownst to me, this had become a tradition established by my predecessor and my "ignorance of the past" caused me to look like an insensitive monster. This grandparent had become accustomed to things being done a certain way, and I became the "scapegoat" when the relative became frustrated with these overwhelming changes in their lives.

When it came to birthdays and holidays, these moments of tension and disapproval seemed to intensify. We were constantly trying to sort through what parts of the past we wanted to retain and what traditions for the future we wanted to establish. This is sensitive territory, let me tell you. No matter how good your intentions may be, someone will inevitably be hurt or offended. It is an inescapable part of blending two families. As hard as I tried to cover what I thought to be all the bases, I still had to absorb the anguish of someone's disapproval from time to time. This was difficult for me as I am sure it will be for you. Essentially though, I realized rather quickly that the ones who criticized the most, were the ones struggling the most. They were still unable to accept us, our children, and the formation of our new family.

As difficult as it may be, try and be as gracious as possible to all your extended family members, even the ones who make it abundantly clear that your union was definitely not their first choice. Allow them opportunities to be involved in the life of your new family. When appropriate, invite them to school plays, ball games, and social gatherings. They, too, need time to bond with each of you. I must make it clear, though, through my own experience and that of others, that there are situations in which a new spouse and the children are forced to deal with the fact that they are not accepted (and may never be) by their spouse's family. I have seen this scenario repeat itself more times than I care to admit since this unfortunate dissension (even if one-sided) affects all parties involved. I will spend an entire chapter later in this book on how best to deal with members of your extended family.

Not only did I experience criticism from my immediate and extended family, I also had to deal with occasional jabs from the outside world. You see, since my style of parenting was inevitably different from that of Karl's former spouse, words of disapproval were quick to come my way when someone didn't agree with the way I was raising Karl's children. And those people were certainly not bashful when it came to sharing their opinions. For example, a year after we were married, Amy entered the seventh grade. Or I should say a new Amy entered the seventh grade. She had decided her passage into adolescence deserved a new look which would include hair that stood seven feet off her head. We fondly nicknamed it "The Wall". Her clothes were loud and funky, and she was nothing like the plain-Jane we once knew. Outrageous was her style and she loved it. She felt self-made and ready to tackle the world.

Now this all happened soon after I arrived so, of course, my parenting skills were called into question by this new form of rebellion (or so they thought). I remember one lady from our church coming up to me during a function and saying, "I can't believe you let her dress that way!" She was appalled at the freedom this one-time Polyanna had been given. What she didn't know (as I did) was the amount of pain this young girl had gone through and how imperative it now was to give her the love and space she needed to discover herself (rags and all). Yes, she was a tad radical, I'll say that, but I knew within my heart she needed room to try on these new hats. So with that in mind, I looked at the lady and simply responded, "Well, she likes it."

I'm sure most families are critiqued by each other at one time or another but for our family, it was like living in a fish bowl. After all, we were not the norm and often felt that we had been singled out as the "ones to watch". It was like having a federal censorship placed on our home. Even our children sensed the supervision of the outside world when it came to their conduct and morals. I remember Katy and Amy complaining after we first blended that "we feel like everyone around us is watching everything we do...they listen to everything we say as if they are trying to find clues to see if we all get along...we hate it." People were curious. They were interested in knowing if we were accepting each other and whether the kids called me "Mom," or Karl, "Dad". We even have had one child pulled out of her Sunday School class by a well-meaning teacher who asked her how she "really" was doing (she was both embarrassed and angry), and we have even had people take our children on outings only to quiz them about any negative feelings they might have about our new family.

Our children have endured a great deal of scrutiny from the outside world over the past twelve years and not all of it has been in a positive light. Some of it has been cruel and insensitive. My husband and I have continually repeated the phrases "let it go" and "forget it" to each of them when they have been bothered by this type of prying and spying. Honestly speaking, we always knew that there were those beyond our doors who truly wanted to see our family bloom while there were those who secretly hoped our family would fail. We have endured their innuendos, their misdiagnoses of our situation, their reams of disapproval, and their outright discrimination. I can tell you that this senseless carping is tremendously taxing on the members of a blended family. They have enough struggles of their own without having to feel watched and judged by their fellowman.

Even though you don't want or need to hear their criticism, please expect it. There is no way of deflecting its fire power. My best advice to you would be two-fold. First, learn to weed out those comments that are legitimately full of wisdom from those which are full of shallow misconceptions and then, most important of all, let these moments go right over your head and not through your heart.

Chapter 8

Start Your Own Traditions

*"You are the best parents anyone could ask
for — I'm glad God put you together."*
Amy

On August 25, 1982, Karl and I, along with my
two children, pulled out of Minneapolis on our journey to
the East Coast. Karl was driving a Ryder truck, bulging
at the seams with all my earthly possessions, and I was
driving our family car stacked with luggage, the children,
and our dog, Boomer.

We had just spent the weekend packing my house
and finishing all the last minute details involved in a
cross-country move. During those three days we enjoyed
a wonderful get-together with my co-workers (they were
some of the most supportive people I have ever known)
and some special family times with my parents, and my
brothers and their families. I can still recall with tears
our send-off dinner. Leaving behind those closest to you

can be especially difficult no matter how bright your future appears.

Our trip to New England seemed especially long since we were driving separate vehicles. If I heard, "Mom, are we almost there yet?" once, I heard it one hundred times as we passed through Indiana, Ohio, and Pennsylvania. After three days on the road, four weary travellers arrived at Karl's restored New England colonial. I was definitely not prepared for what the next 48 hours would hold. The initial greetings were friendly enough but it wasn't until the doors of that moving van were opened did we begin to feel the vibes of tension scanning the atmosphere of our new home.

I cannot put into words the amount of visible anxiety we waded through as we not only blended our children but our household possessions as well. Now remember, we were blending two literal households. That meant we now had, not one, but three couches. This went on to include multiple end tables, lamps, and pictures. As we unpacked the parade of boxes and furniture, we were forced to make the immediate decisions as to what had to be moved, what was to be added and what had to be put away.

One of my most vivid memories of that first day involved moving a dresser in the family room which housed Katy's old Barbie things. If looks could have killed that day, she would have had me four feet under in no time flat. She was both angry and frustrated and had no intention of pretending otherwise. She resented the fact that I was tampering with "her" family's property. Who was I to move her Barbie things from their usual spot? And who was I to come in and change her whole house around? After all, to her, I was still a stranger. She had made no bond with me. From her prospective, I was an intruder.

Even though I knew her diagnosis of me could have best been termed "unfortunate", I tried to be as sensitive as possible toward her and the others as I organized the floor plan of our furniture. Keeping a balance between the "yours" and "mine" seemed imperative at this point. New wallpaper, carpet, and curtains would come later when we were more established.

The kitchen items proved to be an even touchier subject as we were confronted with the fact that we now had two toasters, two blenders, two canister sets, two sets of dishes and two sets of pots and pans. The big question, of course, was whose set was going to be used. Again, realizing the need to keep some of the familiar intact, it was decided to organize the kitchen cabinets to house both sets of dishes in order to provide "freedom of choice" for each of our diners. That might sound like small potatoes to you, but believe me, for the first six months, those kids used only "their" plates when fixing themselves something to eat. (When we ate together, we all used the same plates.) The adoption of universal dinnerware would come at another time and with new mind-sets.

The sign on our door should have read "Lost and Found" since that was exactly what we were experiencing emotionally. While one was losing the privacy of a room, another had found the warmth and companionship of a new sister. While one was struggling with resentment toward these invading "alien forces", another stood quietly by with an invisible banner that read "Welcome Mother".

You see, the sun was both rising and setting on all our worlds. For our children this meant that their time machines no longer allowed them to live in the past. Whether they approved of it or not, they were headed on a new course toward the future. Even for us, as parents, this new course we had vowed to undertake seemed, at best, a bit shaky. We were all on new ground and new territory.

You need to remind yourself when you are knee deep in this kind of "transitional mud", that the goal of oneness within a blended family can only come through the laughter and tears, and through the process of building memories.

Again, I will repeat this important "blended" truth: each child will take these changes differently. Even though this was an extremely troubling time for Katy, our daughter Amy was delighted with my presence and could not have been more cooperative. Her banner of love proved to be very encouraging to me during this assimilation process. And even though Brian had his own set of struggles, the household turf was not a concern to him. Like most boys his age, he was interested in playing with his new friends and exploring his new environment. As for Rachel and Christy, they became immediate friends and played for hours as new sisters. It seems to be that "adaptability" comes easier the younger you are. I learned that even a thirteen-year-old can be set in his or her ways.

Even though our desire was for as smooth a transition as possible, we all struggled with feelings of resentment, frustration, and anxiety at one time or another. As I assess it now, I would call it a time of meeting needs and pulling weeds. The needs to which I am referring were the constant care and development of our new brood; the weeds were those attitudes and emotions which tried to tear down, not build up, our new framework. Confronting those weeds was, at times, an inexhaustible labor of love.

Adjustments came in all shapes and forms for our new family. Even cooking for the evening meal proved to be a perpetual balancing act. Most families become accustomed to having foods served a certain way and our two families were no different. While one family preferred meatballs served plain, the other wouldn't touch them without some sort of sauce. While one preferred lasagna filled with ricotta cheese, cottage cheese would only do for the other. I know this sounds laughable but it was yet another issue that was beating the drums of change. I even got offended (silently, of course) every time my new children didn't like what I served. There were moments when my olive branch began to look a little bare as I constantly offered peace offerings (compromises) to my restless natives.

My stress level was often teetering on overflow and I literally had a headache everyday for the first month (I am prone to migraines anyway). As much as I wanted to make everyone happy, there were days when embracing my new family seemed more like the "Impossible Dream". We were not the Cleavers of the 60's, or the Bradys of the 70's. We were the Andersons of the 80's — the only blended family we knew and somewhat of a mutation to the world around us. My journal reflected these early emotions when I wrote, *"As for everyday living, no one day is ever the same and we face new challenges, demands, and problems daily. Sometimes it seems overwhelming to me and, at other times, it's like we've been together for years."*

I also struggled with feelings of guilt. After all, I had uprooted my children from what had become their home to another area of the country where they now had to share me with four other people. I kept asking myself at times, "Have I been fair to them? Should I have stayed single and weathered the storms of parenting alone?" These and other such questions invaded my inner happiness after I first married.

Moving into Karl's world was difficult for me as found in these words, *"It's hard to have everything so different and have all things belong to Karl and his past...everything is so new for us...at times I resent the fact that they have had to make so few changes compared to my family."* You see, for the most part, Karl's and his children's lives had remained intact. We came to live in their house; we socialized with their friends; we shopped at their supermarket and visited their drug store. Sometimes I felt like we had left everything, and they had left nothing. Of course, this wasn't the whole truth. They had made lots of adjustments as they opened the doors of their lives to three "loons" (State bird) from Minnesota. We were *all* embroiled in the uphill battle of blending, and each of us would hear the chant of trauma at one time or another.

In spite of all we were going through, I realized early on how absolutely vital it was for our new family to begin to establish a new identity for ourselves. I felt it was imperative that we create our own family history and write our own chronicle of recollections. In other words, we needed to collect our own treasury of memories.

Based on this need, I announced during our first Christmas together, that a special shopping day would be planned for each of the children. My mother had always taken me shopping and to lunch during the holidays when I was a child, so I thought this might be a way of adding warm feelings to the relationship I was establishing with my new children. It also served to provide my natural children with the assurance that they still were an important part of my life. I had been working very hard at bonding with my new children, so I am sure my natural children felt a little left behind at times.

Each child was told they could take the entire day off from school, and we would go to the restaurant and stores of their choice. They were delighted with the idea because basically, the entire day was centered on them and them alone. Each one had me all to themselves, and it gave us a wonderful chance to get to know each other a little better. This tradition has continued for years now, the only difference being the price of the meal. When they were young, McDonald's was the first choice. Now it is either Italian, Chinese or Mexican. Intimate feelings are certainly fostered when you share special times such as these.

Another page in our chronicle included our yearly trip to the orchards of western Massachusetts. Since fall is an especially glorious time in New England, we enjoyed the season with a full day of apple picking. We browsed through quaint shops on our way and enjoyed a picnic lunch when we arrived. Since MacIntosh apples are one of our favorites, our children spent hours climbing trees looking for the biggest, reddest finds. After our car was full, we always made our way to the Mill for homemade cider and dumplings. There was nothing like the smell of that old barn. It followed us all the way home. Those were fun days for our new family.

Kodak moments continued through the holidays as we embraced the fellowship of both family and friends. On Christmas Eve, the table was set for twenty or more, a warm fire glowed in the fireplace, and laughter was heard far into the night. The Christmas story was read by one of the children, and we always paused for a time of prayer and praise for all God had done in our lives. This year we added a new touch...the reading of poems and stories which had been written over a century ago.

During Easter, we enjoy an after-church brunch with families we don't get to see that often. The house is full of flowers, the chocolate eggs are in hiding for the little ones and a full buffet of fresh fruit and pastries greets our guests. Spirits are light as we embrace the renewal of spring and celebrate the resurrection of Christ.

I could go on and on with a list of memory-builders that have taken place over the past twelve years. I believe each of these happenings has paved the road toward our successful blending. I would urge you, too, to create your own journal of traditions. These special milestones are the torch with which the "Master Welder" fuses together the reality of oneness. When I hear the words, "Mom, do you remember when...," I know that these events have been forever etched on the walls of their minds in the memory of our family.

Chapter 9

Visitation — An
Emotional Tug-of-War

> *"I like you as my sister. I really miss you*
> *when you go away. I am going to miss*
> *you when I go away. I hope you will not*
> *get lonely."*
>
> Rachel

Just when you believe progress is being made toward building meaningful interpersonal relationships among your flock, another painful adjustment is waiting right around the corner. This is the issue of visitation and its affect on your lives. This was yet another area where my skill as a blended mother could have easily been called into question.

Naively enough, before I was remarried, I believed sharing my new children with their natural parent would hold no emotional pull for me. After all, it was written in the divorce decree, and I had accepted it (or so I thought I would) as part of the package. What I didn't count on was how quickly I was going to become attached to these neat kids. You see, even though I was not their biological mother, I immediately became a mother to them in every sense of the word. I made their meals when they were hungry, I went shopping with them when they needed clothing, I picked up after them when they were messy, I listened to them when they needed to talk, I wiped their tears when they were hurt, and I took care of them when they were sick. Believe me, feelings of love come quickly with this type of caring.

I was totally unprepared for the inevitable day when these same children would kiss me goodbye on their way out the door to spend time with their other mother. Man, was this an adjustment for me. Now I knew that mothers tended to be a jealous and protective breed, but I had no idea I would fit so snugly into this category. Even though I knew (in my head) that they deserved the freedom to leave without my interference, putting my emotions on neutral was a shock to my whole system.

The fear, of course, was that my new children would somehow change toward me after their visitation outing. This observation from my early journal confirms these misgivings, *"When she came home after a week away, she was unbearable and I felt all the ground we had made was just down the drain...after several long talks and lots of tears about her conflicting emotions, we seemed all right and perhaps closer."* I felt deep insecurity in this whole area. I wasn't at all sure how far my new children's loyalty would extend.

After drowning a few times in a sea of anxiety, I quickly came to the conclusion that the only way I was going to survive the unavoidable strain of visitation was to keep the focus off myself and on the needs of my children. After all, I was really a side issue. They were the ones on the front line and their mental welfare was far more important then my need to have them all to myself.

It was clear to me from the very beginning of our life together that each of our children was wrestling with a number of conflicting emotions. They were entangled in a major inner struggle which centered around the question, "Where do the familiar (natural parent) and the new (adopted parent) fit into my life?" (This is even true of a child whose parent has died.) And they are processing with regularity such questions as, "Is it all right for me to love my new parent?", and, "By so doing, am I being disloyal to my natural parent?" I always believed my children basically wanted to be fair and open, but even for them, these were weighty and difficult issues.

Since I had been brought up in a home where "freedom", in terms of personal discovery, resounded with booming clarity, I knew the importance of allowing our children the emotional freedom to piece together, for themselves, the many pieces of their new family puzzle. For my husband and me, this meant a total verbal "blackout" on any criticism we might have of our former spouses. This also meant a continual "sealing of the lips" when we felt the tendency to use an innuendo (or two) in order to find fault with their departed parent. Keep in mind that if you give in to the urge to censure or condemn the other parent, you are putting your child in the uncomfortable position of having to defend that parent. Even if your former spouse is less than an ideal parent (either by ignoring your child or living a lifestyle you find offensive), it is still important not to openly find fault. In a nutshell, we made the decision to keep our mouths shut and let our children find their own answers to these probing questions.

As I said before, each of your children will put the pieces of their family puzzle together differently. For example, one of our daughters told me, a year or so after we were married, that she had decided to put each of us in "boxes" in her mind. She explained that this helped her keep us distinctively different in terms of our emotional meaning and the roles we would play in her life, at least for the time being. It was only with time that our children learned to mark, with clarity, their own parameters for these multi-faceted relationships, thus lessening the tension in this whole area.

I have come to believe though, that most, if not all, of the pain these children experience in the area of visitation comes directly from the parents themselves (natural or blended). Parents are the ones contributing to this emotional tug-of-war by means of a powerful tool called "guilt". In Dr. David D. Burns' book, <u>Feeling Good — The New Mood Therapy</u>, he explains that "guilt is the emotion we experience when we have the following thoughts: 1) I have done something I shouldn't have (or I have failed to do something I should have) because my actions fall short of my moral standards and violates my concept of fairness, and 2) this "bad behavior" shows that I am a bad person (or that I have an evil streak or a tainted character or a rotten core, etc.)."

For the blended child, dealing with a manipulative custodial or natural parent, this can translate: 1) I feel guilty because I should have gone with my natural parent or (I shouldn't have left my custodial parent) and basically, my actions seem to always fall short of both my

104

parents' desires, and 2) I must be a bad person. Why do I keep hurting everyone? Let me illustrate this point. Some years ago, one of our daughters had been invited by her natural parent to do something special with that parent for the day. I was working in the kitchen when the call came so I heard my daughter say she would rather make it another time. When the room grew silent and she started to pace, I knew her words had been met with great resistance. When she got off the phone, she looked at me and said, "Am I that bad?" Guilt covered her face like a Halloween mask. You see, she hadn't lived up to the expectations of one of her parents. Because of that, she had now been sentenced to walk the plank of guilt.

Too often the children of blended families are emotionally black-mailed by Moms and Dads who are trying to gain control. They manipulate their children with looks, tears, innuendoes, and silence. They use these tactics to show their disapproval of their children's actions and decisions. Sadly enough though, the more coercive these parents become, the more damage, emotionally speaking, they inflict on their children. The ransom for this type of blackmail is "emotional instability" and because of this, there are days, months, and even years of tenseness before and after visitation. Notes from my journal substantiate these feelings when I wrote, *"They had a hard time leaving this week,"* and *"There were many tears when they returned about their conflicting feelings."*

This type of parental behavior is wrong and should be avoided at all costs. Even if you are witnessing this type of manipulation, *do not* (I repeat, do not) participate in this game. Give your children the emotional freedom they deserve. In order for them to balance the highs and lows of this emotional friction, they will need your love, not your disfavor; your support, not your suspended approval; your prayers, not your depreciative remarks. Practically speaking, this means that when your child asks to see the other parent, your approval should be given non-grudgingly and with as much good will as possible. Of course, there are situations when a request does not coincide with what the custodial parent feels is in the best interest of the child, but compromises should always be made to try and accommodate both parties.

The truth is that, even in the best of situations, these children are easily afflicted with feelings of frustration (keeping everyone happy), resentment (angry that they were put in this situation), animosity (unwilling to adapt to their new home), and at times, outrage (they feel their life is a disaster) during those early laps of blending. Very often, it is the blended family which deals with the aftermath of a short temper, a disagreeable attitude, a sour disposition, or a series of crying jags. Let me warn you...picking up the pieces of an emotionally torn child is no picnic and will require great sensitivity and wisdom. You must be careful not to become resentful when you feel you have somehow become your new child's wailing wall or punching bag. Again, try to keep the focus off yourself and on the innumerable needs of your child.

Personally speaking, for the most part, I was able to "put a lid" on the compulsive urge I sometimes felt to try to control my children's responses and behavior toward the natural parent. But in all honesty, there were times when my own insecurities and fears got the best of me. I served subtle tones of disapproval like a tennis pro serves aces. I found that using a trusted friend as a sounding board was both helpful (perspective-wise) and therapeutic (healing-wise) when my frustration level got out of control. I would challenge you to do the same.

It is also important to realize that visitation not only affects the departing child but the entire family as well. The reason for this is two-fold. First of all, the physical closeness you share is put on hold, even if just for two hours. Something has changed. Someone is missing. Even in a large family like ours, when one is missing, a void is felt by all. At one time or another, I'm sure we all pondered the same question, "Will they return the same way they left or will they somehow have changed toward our family?"

When Rachel and Christy were very young, Christy went to Minnesota for a week of visitation. After being gone only a few days, Rachel came to me and said, "Mom, I don't like being the only little one in the house." They had become close in that short time and she missed the companionship of her new sister. In fact, the quote you read under the title of this chapter came from a letter Rachel wrote Christy before she left. In it she said, "I like you as my sister. I really miss you when you go away. I am going to miss you when I go away. I hope you will not get lonely." You see, visitation not only affects the departing child but those who are left behind.

Second, it has been our experience, as well as of many others living in similar situations, that it usually takes two or three days for the visiting child to adjust back into their normal routine. They can either walk through the door like a vacationer just back from Disney

World or a wounded pup straight from the pound. Of course, the ideal profile would be that of a child *learning to adjust* to the new family situation with the love and support of both sets of parents. This to me, though, seems to be the exception, not the rule.

There are too many cases where a part-time parent insists on playing Santa Claus for the weekend, thus making it difficult on the child when they are forced to adjust back to the reality of dishes, homework, and limited television. One family I spoke with recently, said they counted on at least 48 hours of "off the wall behavior" after their son's weekend Christmas adventure.

Or I have seen the reverse happen also. A child can be so barraged with negative comments about the custodial family, that they arrive home bruised and beaten emotionally. This happened to one of our daughters years ago when she was on a visitation weekend. It so happened that she was playing a question and answer game with her natural parent one afternoon, when the question came up, "What one name would you never name your child?" Much to the child's surprise, the name the parent used was that of the child's new sister. She was quick to recall this incident as soon as she came through the door. Her story ended with this statement, "Mom, they knew that was my sister's name. They just said that to hurt me." It worked. She had been hurt.

In closing, I believe there are two things you can do, as a blended parent, to provide an atmosphere of love and support for your children during this time. First, give them lots of space and be ready to be a good listener. When your child returns from these excursions, don't bombard them with questions. If the child seems upset, quiet or withdrawn, let them know you are aware of the difficulty they may be experiencing and that you are available to talk when and if they are ready. Try to build a safe place for them to communicate (if they so choose) by building a foundation of genuine love. It has been my experience that when I respected their freedom to unwind, an honest, free-flowing interaction was often the result.

And secondly, and most important of all, *pray* your children through this ragged time of sensitivity, for *God is the only one who can heal torn emotions!*

Chapter 10

The Value of
Authentic Friendships

"Thanks for being my friend. I love our
relationship. I cherish it."

Sonnie

Finding creative and unique greeting cards has always been a favorite challenge of mine and some time ago, I found a simple, but eloquent card with the following quote engraved on its cover, "The better part of one's life consists of his friendships". It had been penned by Abraham Lincoln some 200 years ago. Now I had always believed the sentiment behind these words but it wasn't until I blended families that I realized the significance of these cohorts, companions, and confidantes and their essential part in helping us build a positive new life. In fact, I shudder to think of what life would have been like without them.

Fortunately for me, Karl's closest friends at the time of our marriage showed immediate support for our new family. I hadn't expected this type of acceptance since most of the second marriages I had observed in the past seldom remained in the friendships of their former lives. Their new life usually meant a new set of friends. Since I had half-way prepared myself for having to do the same, I was truly surprised by their instant willingness to include me and my children into their lives.

This chapter is not only about this one particular couple but about a number of other cherished friends who have encouraged us individually and enriched our overall home life in a number of significant ways over the past twelve years. There are four specific areas where the value of their friendship impacted our lives.

Our friends refreshed and encouraged us. So often when we were overwhelmed with the tremendous pressures of each day, they were the ones who provided a much needed "relaxative". Their invitations to socialize directly contributed to our mental health in a vital way. Their good-humored companionship gave us a breather from the heavy responsibilities involved in blending two families. And the warmth of their hospitality added grit to our character and stamina to our temperament when we were listing from the challenge of keeping one step ahead of our united forces.

Most of our friends are great adventurers who are ready to try anything new. Our times together ranged from an elegant dinner in Boston to a night of games around our kitchen table. We built a wonderful sense of camaraderie as we barbecued, bowled, and played miniature golf together. The fellowship we enjoyed during these times became invaluable to our own well-being. Over the years we have spent weeks skiing in New Hampshire and sunbathing in Florida with one couple in particular. It was during these types of gatherings that we were able to vent the layers of frustration and disappointment that had been piling up internally. We conversed on all levels from the idle sound of chit chat to the soliloquy of sharing our inner thoughts and ideas. The solace we found in the circle of their company strengthened our mental and emotional endurance levels. Moreover, our friends not only provided encouragement and refreshment by their physical presence but by the written word as well. The notes and cards I discovered in my mailbox often provided a sense of courage and resolve when the valleys before me seemed especially low. Even when their observations were less than accurate, confidence and perseverance were added to my heart-of-hearts when I received such notes as "I have watched you adjust so beautifully and graciously cope with every little happening (little did she know)." Cyclones of stress were often calmed by cards that read, "We realize you are going through a difficult time and we hope it helps to know we care," or "I hope you know that I would like to be a friend you can depend on." These expressions of concern and their desire to help planted my feet in a bed of deep determination to make this marriage work.

Our friends listened to us and offered perspective.
After we were first married, I became very friendly with the wife of Karl's closest friend and often found myself calling her with tears that cried, "I am so discouraged today. Nothing seems to be going as I had expected and everyday there seems to be something new. It is either another conflict, another hurt or another obstacle to overcome. I really don't think I'm doing a very good

job." After hearing the specifics of a heart in turmoil, her quick, concise and very assuring comeback always sounded something like this: "You are doing just fine...you really are making progress, believe me...those kids are responding to you and each other in a very positive way...you just can't see it because you are right in the middle of it...someday they'll see how much you love them and all you are doing to prove that love."

She did two things for me during those conversations. First, she listened to me. This meant, as Webster puts it, she heard me with thoughtful action. She gave me her ear. She tuned in to my channel. She gave me her time. She offered herself as a willing target for my daily blasts of burdens. Her continual expressions of affirmation brought a resurgence of strength and hope to my fatigued frame. I discovered her significant role in my life when I wrote these words after only four months of marriage, *"I really like her and am, so glad for her friendship in my life now."* When you are engulfed in the quicksand of changing emotions, it is so important that you ventilate your anxieties, fears, and concerns with someone you can trust.

Second, she, along with many others, gave me the gift of perspective. You see, when you become overwhelmed by your situation (and this will happen, I assure you), and you begin to feel a bit sizzled around the edges, your focus has the tendency to become blurry and distorted. What were deep convictions can become confusing questions and what were absolutes can now become negotiables. You begin to identify with the man on television who walks around lopsided until he has had his

114

"V-8"! You feel off-balance, and the world in which you find yourself seems rather dubious.

You have, what I fondly refer to, as "Acute Perspectinitis". This is an emotional condition where the person loses their capacity to view things in their proper importance and relevance. They focus only on the immediate crisis of their life and forget to survey the depth and distance of the whole picture. They zero in on the failures of their situation and cease to see the successes they have logged along the way. The person majors in minor issues and dwells on the negatives rather than the positives. This condition, if gone unchecked, can bring depression, discouragement and a feeling of despair.

At one time or another, we have all suffered from this emotional virus. To my knowledge, the only cure available is large doses of perspective from the people who know us well. I was fortunate enough to receive these injections from both my family and friends. They were the people who were willing to provide an accurate picture of the arena before me when my own eyes were swollen and bruised from hurt and disillusionment. When all I could see around me were the ugly weeds of resistance, they were the ones who reminded me of the budding flowers within our relationships. And when all I could hear was the constant sparring of warring children, they spot-lighted small ways in which true bonding was indeed taking place. Their common admonitions of "You've forgotten how far you have come," or "You've become blind to the strides your family has made," did for me what "V-8" did for the lopsided man. By helping me find perspective, they gently restored my vision.

Our friends gave us a sense of community. With my own family living fifteen-hundred miles away, the physical companionship these folks offered became indispensable to me. My mother and I are very close, and we talk often by phone, but the distance always makes it difficult to recount in detail the specifics of who, what, when and where on a regular basis. And as much as she yearned to hug me on those dark days, "AT&T's Reach Out and Touch" didn't have arms. For this reason especially, the sense of community extended to us by these dear people sometimes felt like the "feathers and wings" David talks about in Psalms when He describes the shelter of God. Psalms 91:4 says, "He will cover you with His feathers and under His wings you will find refuge." We not only found shelter in the refuge of God but in the arms of His people as well. They have brought into our lives a sense of security and belonging.

Not only did these friends become priceless for us as a couple, but they were extremely helpful to our children as they sought acceptance in the world outside our doors. Their sheer presence in our lives yielded a positive response of recognition and approval for the children individually as well as our new family. The warmth of this recognition played well to that eight-year-old boy trying to find his way in a whole new world and to that twelve-year-old gal encountering not only a new mother but the awkwardness of adolescence.

Before I married Karl, he and his friends enjoyed a standing tradition of sharing Sunday dinners together at their favorite restaurants, which we continued long after we were married. Our fellowship continued through the day at one another's homes and often went on late into the evening. As the adults enjoyed yet another cup of coffee and goodies, the teenagers would crash in the privacy of their bedrooms while the younger ones used this play time to create theatre masterpieces. They wrote, directed, and acted in a variety of different plays as well as choreographed dazzling dance recitals! Our collection of costumes and dress-up clothes were used to disguise the stars. I cannot tell you the number of productions we sat through but, suffice to say, we became seasoned theatre-goers. When they were tired of that, they used their wonderful imaginations to set-up make-believe offices, stores, and restaurants. My home always resembled a freshman boy's dorm room when they were finished. These and other such moments with old and new friends have provided us with security, consistency, and first-rate memories.

Speaking of memories, I need to share with you, on a lighter note, one such event when I questioned whether the companionship of friends was worth the expense, physically and emotionally speaking! We had only been married a few months when Karl and his friends informed me that not only did they eat Sunday meals together, but they also skied together one week each year. I need to tell you that this announcement brought on an instant panic attack. I hadn't been on skis since I was a freshman in high school and, at that time, I fell coming down an "advanced" slope (which I had no business being on) and spent two weeks in the hospital and two months in physical therapy. But since I wanted to please both my husband and my children, I agreed to try skiing at least one more time. Getting ready for this trip should have tipped me off that this was going to be anything but restful. Remember now, I needed to have enough clothes for all seven of us plus the array of ski pants, boots, hats, and mittens we would need for seven days.

Our friends had rented a small house in ski country with just three small bed-rooms and two bath-rooms for all seventeen of us! Yes, I said seventeen! The kitchen table only sat six people so we ate in three shifts. Our day began at 6:30 am when we rose to prepare breakfast for seventeen, make lunches for seventeen and transport seventeen to the slopes by 9:00 a.m. After putting our youngest three children into ski school each day, my husband and I would head for the easiest slopes for my daily lesson. There were times when I literally cried coming down those mountains. When we returned home, a complete dinner had to be served, and by 7:00 p.m., I was ready for bed! This continued for seven days straight. I thought I was going to die! I often wondered whether I should have been grateful that Karl's friends had accepted me or perhaps I should have hoped they hated me! Of course, I say all this in jest. They were wonderful friends to us both and we will always be grateful for their love and support.

Our friends prayed for us. So many times over the past twelve years, these same friends have whispered in our ears the words, "We are praying for you." In essence, they were making a commitment to commune with God on our behalf. Their petitions have brought into our lives a sense of peace and comfort in the midst of some troubling situations. Even though we, ourselves, were praying daily for our family, it was such an encour-agement to know we had prayer partners waiting in the wings. More times than I can recall, we have walked together before the throne of God with such requests as, "Lord, develop within these relationships a measure of deep love and establish a bond of unity within this new home."

When specific problems arose, we were quick to alert our prayer chain, which consisted of both friends and family, since we knew they were as confident as we were in the power of prayer. They also shared our belief that no matter how noble our intentions or how vigorous our efforts, our family would never flourish without the help of God. We are living proof of God's intervention and power. Those collective prayers made the difference between a forced co-existence and a consenting alliance based on love. We are in debt to those prayer warriors whose knees have become worn on our behalf.

As you perform your own production of "Married With Children", you, too, will need an audience in the balcony of your lives to applaud your efforts and to provide the emotional backing needed at times for the show to go on. Sometimes it is easy for a blended family to immediately surround itself with good, supportive friends but unfortunately, this is the exception, not the rule. Too often, blended families are treated as castaways on a deserted island.

If you find the world outside your doors holding you at arm's length, I would encourage you, then, to make the first move. By this I mean, single out those people with whom you feel most comfortable and then think of ways to introduce them to your new family. Inviting them to your home for dinner, sharing a community activity together, or even looking for ways to meet a specific need in their life are a few ways to transform an acquaintance into a friend. Remember, to be a friend is to make a friend.

In time, these balcony people can become, as an Arabian proverb puts it, "Friends with whom one may pour out one's heart, chaff and grain together, knowing that the gentlest of hands will take and sift it, keep what is worth keeping and with a breath of kindness, blow the rest away." While looking through old school papers of each of the children, I found a worksheet of Brian when he was just nine years old that asked the question, "What type of friend would you make?" His humble response was, "I am an unselfish, helpful, kind, and thoughtful friend with a wonderful sense of humor. You are bound to like me." How very true that is of the people who have entered our lives and become our friends. Their tremendous love and support for our family will never be forgotten. To each and every one of them, we graciously dedicate these words, "The Lord blessed our lives when He gave us friends like you."

Chapter 11

Meanwhile Back at the Church

"In the last week it's really hit me how important it is to be a real Christian ...open-minded and not chained down to legality. I never realized how many people are really bogged down — it's too bad."

Katy

Even though our closest supporters were Christians and we all attended the same church, the community of believers, as a whole, simply did not know what to do with us. A quote from Joyce Landorf Heatherley's book, Unworld People, describes the response we experienced as a blended family. "For the Christian, not only is the divorce a living, on-going hell but during the time preceding and following it, when the couple is the most seriously wounded, a new and tortuous episode begins. Their emotions are repeatedly stabbed by the rejection, criticism, and ostracism which comes from the church and the body of believers."

These words are not an exaggeration or an over-statement. They are a true portrayal of the plight of many blended families across this country when it comes to finding sanctuary in the organized church. For me personally, they are a painful reminder of our own struggle to find acceptance in our local place of worship. My journal says it best when I wrote, *"At times I feel 'shut out' by the people at church and that is one thing I am trying to adjust to."*

I had no idea how difficult it was going to be for our new family when it came to assimilation into the body of believers. I never imagined encountering such blatant rejection or such intentional ostracism. I didn't realize how powerful those subtle teachings of "conditional" love had become within the Church. Even though the Scriptures call for an "unconditional" love among believers, somewhere along the way, this command had been rewritten to include stipulations. The culprits are well-meaning, misguided Christians who have superimposed their own set of standards with which to show this kind of unconditional love. In other words, their mercy has it bounds. They rationalize this attitude by saying, "How can I really love this person when I disagree with their behavior." Even though they know they worship a forgiving God, they seem unwilling to follow His example. Sadly enough, I have seen the Christian community embrace an ex-murderer and their family more quickly than they would the divorced person and their family.

I found people, for the most part, falling into one of four categories when it came to dealing with our family. I refer to the first group of people as God's self-appointed "Whips". They were relatively small in number but their relentless, unforgiving spirit constantly seemed to haunt us. They felt it was their responsibility to preside over the decisions of our life as both judge and jury, and their sentence always included the words, "Guilty As Charged". They seldom had the courage to pronounce this verdict to our faces but their entire demeanor and proverbial comments gave them away. The next group of individuals, though somewhat larger, are quite similar to the "Whips" but not quite as harsh. Unlike their counterparts, they were interested in hearing the whole story. In fact, they wanted to know all the sordid details of our previous lives. They needed to be convinced that our remarriage was based on "Biblical grounds". If, in their opinion, it was not, they had no qualms about sentencing us outside their loving, caring community.

The third group is the largest of all, and I refer to these people as the "Tolerators". They were the ones who had basically decided to stay out of this whole theological debate. The only thing they knew for sure was that we didn't fit into their mold. In other words, they tolerated our existence. They made it crystal clear that we were not one of them, nor would we ever be. The reality of our situation caused them discomfort and they avoided our company at all costs. This mentality was the hardest for me personally.

And lastly, thank God, there were those "fellow strugglers" in Jesus Christ who believed in the words forgiveness, grace, and restoration. Their unconditional love and support gave authenticity to their walk with Christ. I don't know if we would have ever stayed in the organized church without these true disciples.

The scorn we experienced during those early years ranged from outright public opposition to our marriage to a decision by the leadership of our church to strip me of my teaching privileges. We had even been told by some that they had no interest in being our friends. The words, "We do not want to socialize with you and Karl," left me numb for days. These are just a few of the numerous incidents when we felt the bristled backs of God's people.

We were like the man in the parable of the Good Samaritan. We had been beaten by the circumstances of life in ways few people could ever understand and, instead of being acknowledged and embraced, we were ignored and abandoned. Of course, this wasn't true of all God's people but the majority found it easier to walk to the other side of the road, just as the priest and Levite had done. The few Samaritans who did show compassion chose, by their actions, to see our wounds and feel our pain.

I remember a pastor friend of ours coming for a visit and asking the inevitable question, "Why have you folks decided to stay at Emmanuel (fictitious name)? Hasn't it been incredibly difficult?" A resounding "Yes" came from both our lips. We shared with him the number of times during that first year when we stood quietly alone after church waiting for someone to speak to us (besides those close, personal friends I referred to earlier). We recalled the tears that had been shed over episodes where separation and exclusion had left their mark on our lives.

But we also verbalized our inner resolve to confront these doors of divorced and remarried prejudice. After all, this segment of family life was not a secular phenomenon nor was it a disease of the pagans. Its devastation would eventually touch the Church and its brokenness would someday strike its members. We wanted to be part of a movement within the Body of Christ who reached out to these walking wounded. After all, if the Church didn't try to meet the overwhelming needs of these dear people and their children, we were certain they would seek refuge elsewhere. Their needs were that great. And since we had felt, firsthand, the pain of divorce and were now learning the ropes of blending, walking away was not an option for us.

This decision took place almost twelve years ago. Though much progress has been made toward embracing the divorced and remarried in mainline evangelical churches, an incident that occurred at a women's retreat at which I was speaking recently, reminded me, once again, that the battle was far from over. We had just been seated for the noon meal when the director came over and asked me to give a brief synopsis of my afternoon workshop. I explained that my material would deal specifically with practical insights and guidelines (as well as personal discoveries) for the divorced, the single parent, the blended family mother, and the Christian supporter whom God would use to encourage these women.

When I returned to my table, the lady seated next to me immediately proceeded to tell me and the other women seated at our table a story about a couple from her church who had divorced and left the church. Sometime later, one of them returned with a new spouse and family. Her entire demeanor told me that she had somehow deciphered my words to mean that I had been sent here to crusade against the plague of divorce and remarriage. Feeling she had found an ally, her tone became more indignant as she ended with these words, "And this man thought we should have accepted him and his new family back into our fellowship...Can you believe that?" Sadness, not anger, filled my heart as I answered quietly, "It's hard to believe." Her words were tragic and her body language devastating. If there was anyone in that entire room that needed to hear the message of my workshop, it was this woman. Of course, she never came.

I had made a pledge to myself before we were married that, for the first year, all my energies would be directed toward my new family — there would be no extra-curricular activities. To this day, I am so glad I kept this promise because the pressures and commitments of boards, clubs, or committees would have sapped the inner resources needed for my new post as wife, mother, housekeeper, chief cook and bottle washer, laundress, nurse, chauffeur, psychologist, and referee.

Eventually, though, I started to entertain old friends as well as new ones and began lunching with people I really enjoyed. My inner craving for companionship was reflected in these words from my journal, *"I desperately need their fellowship and hope these friendships will grow."* It was during those times of socializing that these heavenly bodies got a first hand look at our developing family. As they were introduced to the individuality of its members, they witnessed the global warming taking place on our planet. By opening the doors of our hearts and our home, we allowed them the opportunity to eyewitness the cultivation of our growing relationships. They came to appreciate the uniqueness of our situation and in time, even began to visibly root for the success of our union. I recorded this sentiment in December of

1983 when I wrote, "*it seems so much more comfortable with the people from church...so much easier...people are finally warming up.*" Another notation from my journal reinforced this warming trend as found in these words, "*We have come along way in the eyes of the people at church...they seem more friendly and supportive.*" In fact, some of my better memories go back to an afternoon some five years ago when a friend of mine acknowledged her one-time verbal protest to our pastor over the "inappropriateness" of my teaching a Sunday School class on "Divorce." Over coffee, this woman expressed her personal regret for that action since she now felt she possessed a better understanding of the ministry capabilities of the divorced within the church. I admired her courage to apologize to me personally and desperately appreciated her willingness to be enlightened by the Word of God.

Even though the type of behavior to which I have been referring has no biblical grounds whatsoever, its power to puncture the fragile emotions of blended family members is undeniable. This scenario, if repeated often enough, creates a perfect breeding ground for the destructive emotions of bitterness and resentment. They creep into lives like fog on a rainy night, and once entrenched, can interfere with the infrastructure of these delicate relationships.

If you are presently encountering the segregation and ostracism of other Christians, then you are a prime candidate for the offense of these subtle, but controlling emotions. In order to ward off these "menaces of the heart", you must learn to live the role of the "victor", rather than that of a "victim". This can be done by concentrating on God, His Word, and the needs of others. Allow me to be more specific.

The first thing you must do is to constantly *keep your eyes focused on God and not His people.* We humans give far too much credence to the responses of our brother, rather than to the opinion of our God. We play our lives out in dependence of the affirmation of others, instead of the unconditional acceptance of our Lord. We must resist this tendency to put the child before the Father. After all, God's people are still unfinished pieces of clay in the hands of the Potter. They are not completed works of art. We get into trouble spiritually when we lay the expectations we have of our Father at the feet of His children. This will always lead to disappointment.

Though Christians bear the resemblance of their Father, they pale in comparison when it comes to the ability to meet our every need. He alone is qualified for that job. We must be careful not to place our confidence before the wrong throne. I cannot emphasize this truth enough. It is imperative that you and I center our lives around Christ and His approval and not around His people and their version of acceptance.

Second, you must allow His word "to be a lamp to your feet and a light for your path." (Psalms 119:105) You will find encouragement for your soul as you read the stories of men and women just like you who have found new beginnings through the graciousness of God. The promises you will discover within its pages bring a ground swell of hope when you are walking through the unending valley of adjustments. When you read such verses as "He is able to do immeasurably more than we ask or imagine, according to His power who is at work in us" (Eph. 3:20), and "No eye has seen, no ear has heard, no mind has conceived what God has prepared for those who love Him" (I Corn. 2:9), you will be reminded once again that God does have the power to unite your new family.

Third, it is important that you begin to involve yourself in the lives of other struggling individuals. As deep as your own waters may seem, there are those within your world who are not only wading in a sea of pain, but are literally drowning. Life, for whatever reason, has given them a heavy and bleeding heart. They are in need of the soft touch of a helping hand, the warm smile of a caring face, the attentive ears of an earnest listener and the soothing words of a concerned supporter. They need you, my friend.

You see, by choosing to be concerned with the needs of others, you deflect attention away from your own pain. Paul spoke of this creative use of pain when he wrote, "What a wonderful God we have — He is the Father of our Lord Jesus Christ, the source of every mercy, and the One who so wonderfully comforts and strengthens us in our hardships and trials. And why does He do this? That when others are troubled, needing our sympathy and encouragement, we can pass on to them this same help and comfort God has given us." (II Corn. 1:3, Living Letters)

Please understand, my reflection of the past comes only out of a deep desire to be constructive. My introspection is meant to inspire change. The type of behavior to which I have referred is wrong and ought not to be part of the Body of Christ. The Bible gives us a clear-cut mandate to love God first and then our neighbor. Sometimes though, I think we become a bit vague on what it really means to love that neighbor. Vine's Exposition of Biblical Words explanation says it best, "Christian love, whether exercised toward the brethren, or toward men generally, is not an impulse from the feelings, it does not always run with the natural inclinations, nor does it spend itself only upon those for whom some affinity is discovered. Love seeks the welfare of all...works no ill to any ...love seeks opportunity to do good to all men and especially toward them that are of the household of the faith."

What this means to me personally is that when I see someone in need, whether it be emotional, spiritual, or physical, I am to do my best to meet that need. It is an act of my will and not of my emotions, and it is to be played out without my censorship. In relation to blended families, this means that it is the responsibility of the local body with whom this family worships to take the time to listen to that Mom or Dad when they are showing definite signs of "Overload". It means involving themselves in the lives of their children through a walk in the park or a day on the beach. It means including them in a social activity that has traditionally just been for their group of friends.

I am convinced that Christ longs for His people to get serious about His command to accept one another, care for one another, build-up one another, forgive one another, stimulate one another, submit to one another, serve one another, carry one another's burdens, and be patient with one another. He is, in essence, asking each of us to emerge ourselves in the lives of those around us — whether they be broken, blended, or whole.

Chapter 12

Request Impartiality From Your Extended Family

"If you are willing, I want to try and have a good relationship with you. It will take time and patience."

Amy

Before giving my first seminar on blended families, I called my mother who lives in the Midwest, to go over the highlights of my material. She listened patiently as I unfolded a lengthy summation of the truths I had learned during my twelve years inside a blended family. "Sharon," she finally said, "you have forgotten something very important — the role of grandparents, aunts, and uncles within your new family." How right she was and how glad I was she had remembered it for me. This book wouldn't be complete without an honest discussion on the vital role of the extended family and its potential affect on the blended home.

As in the area of visitation, this was yet another phase of family life for which I was totally unprepared. I had spent little time unearthing the possible struggles we would encounter while incorporating our extended families into our lives. Or perhaps growing up with *"The Brady Bunch"* had left me with the impression that the only problems facing a blended family would come from within their own home. After all, this popular sitcom seldom addressed the kind of sensitive issues that often arise when extended family members are introduced to the "yours, mine, and ours" concept of a blended family. They never seemed to deal with the hundreds of hot buttons that typically plague these new relationships. It was as if Mike, Carol and Company lived on a deserted island.

Even though the Bradys were, of course, a fictitious family, they were the only blended family with which I had ever really been acquainted. As one of their faithful viewers, I had been brainwashed into believing that blended life was a piece of cake and that all would be well at the end of each day, just like it was at the end of each show. Not only that, I had foolishly come up with the mistaken notion that any reservations our relatives might have had over our union would immediately dissolve once our marriage took place. Talk about naive. I was in for one rude awakening. It certainly didn't take me long to realize that none of these lofty expectations (perhaps a better word would be *fantasies*) would become reality in my life. No, our children did not fall in love with each other overnight and yes, there were members of our extended family who were less than thrilled with our existence.

My wonderful bubble of innocence was quickly deflated by a variety of explosive adjustments that took place when we began to replace customs of the past with traditions for the future. It hasn't been until recently that I have finally come to understand why we continually seemed to lock horns with some of the members of our extended family. What I didn't realize was that the formation of our new home meant, for them, an end to a family era. The family they once knew would never again be the same. The history and traditions they shared would now be a thing of the past. Our new family meant change and lots of it.

Our perspective, on the other hand, was quite different from theirs. Our marriage meant the beginning of a brand new life. We had no desire to live in the past and were excited about the changes that would take place in our new family. As you can see, we were both coming from two different ends of the spectrum and this, in and of itself, accounted for a great deal of the tension we experienced during those early years. I wish I had possessed this type of insight at the beginning of our life together, for I surely would have exercised far greater sensitivity in the way in which I approached these delicate relationships and in the way I handled what seemed to be words of disapproval or acts of rejection.

This is not to say, however, that we would have lived "incident-free" lives either. In fact, it is my personal belief that no matter how honorable my intentions, how pure my motives, or how tactful my approach may have been, there were going to be moments when we would inevitably feel the effects of stress, strain and tension within these relationships. A recent reflection of my own past struggles has helped me further identify a number of other reasons why some of these relationships are able to grow and flourish and why others fizzle and die. These sobering glimpses have helped me understand from where these feelings of uneasiness and apprehension come and why these relationships are so often plagued by bitter conflict.

In order to set the tone for this frank discussion, it is important for you to remember that just as the members of a blended family responded differently to the bonding process, so will it be with the extended family member. Some of them will be able to take immediate steps toward embracing your new family, while others will stand poised and ready to flex the ultimate cold shoulder. I know our own family can identify with both of these responses. Through the years, the recognition we have received has ranged from a strong flow of warmth and acceptance to a churning current bent on keeping us at an emotional arms length. And even though some of our children have been able to build some very special and meaningful relationships with grandparents, aunts and uncles, we have others who have literally given up on ever belonging to their new parent's family. At one time or another, we have all ridden a carousel of emotions when it came to dealing with the members of our extended families. This unending rotation has been filled with soundbites of tears and laughter, misunderstandings and compromises, and periods of acceptance and rejection.

Here again, we find the children of blended families asking the same question, "Am I wanted here?" but this time it is directed toward a different audience — their new extended family. I well remember being eyewitness to the reticence of each of my own children as they watched for positive and negative feedback in answer to that one question. Until they began to feel vibes of acknowledgement, interest, and concern, they were reluctant to allow these virtual strangers into their lives. Because of this, I have come to believe that the reason many of these relationships never seem to get off the ground has more to do with the role of the adult than it does with the role of the child. It is the adult, by virtue of age and maturity, who is clearly the one setting the emotional tone. The blended child will just reciprocate whichever sentiment is sent their way. A greeting filled with hearty enthusiasm will be returned with a warm, inviting smile. Likewise, an encounter of indifference will prompt a blast of emotional distance. Very seldom have I witnessed a blended child rejecting the sincere efforts of an extended family member. Of course, there are exceptions to this truth but, for the most part, these children have a real willingness to establish a meaningful tie with their new parent's family.

Now if this is true, you may be asking yourself, "Then why would an adult be unwilling to take the lead and go full speed ahead with these new relationships?" The answer lies, sadly enough, in what they believe to be the importance of the "natural" versus the "blended" child. You see, there are a large number of adults who place great value in the case of "flesh and blood". They believe the genetic link alone holds the highest value in a family tie. This mind-set espouses the belief that the biological connection is the one and only basis for any type of enduring bond.

When this type of logic is played out to the children of a blended family, it will translate into an automatic tendency on the part of the extended family member to openly prefer the natural over the blended child. There is nothing more damaging to these relationships than this type of bigotry. The decision to play favorites based on blood type alone truly delays any hope of developing a sense of rapport between these individuals. Now while this sentiment may hold great significance in the minds of adults, it means very little to a child seeking matching identity within their new extended family.

I can still hear the words of one of our children after a family gathering years ago. "Mom," she said, "don't they realize we are one family now? They can't be warm to one of us and cold to another. Don't they realize how much that hurts us?" She had so wanted to be accepted by her new relatives but was constantly being preempted by her "natural" sister. Sadly enough, I don't think these people ever really understood how their favoritism affected our children.

At the beginning of our life together, Karl and I requested of both families that our children be treated on an equal basis. Practically speaking, this would mean that if they gave one child ten dollars on their birthday, then all would receive the same amount on theirs. And if one was invited to share a special meal out with a grandparent, then each would eventually be included in the same ritual. Of course, this was the easy part since it just involved the act of outward giving. Most people can abide by such specific requests. The difficulty would come when the giving required an exercise of the heart, not the pocketbook. You see, I could insist that my mother stuff the correct dollar bill in the birthday envelope but I could never force her into loving her new grandchild nor could I demand that my brothers reach out to their new niece. They were the ones who had to make the conscious decision to abandon any sense of sibling prejudice and stand ready, willing, and able to build strong and lasting relationships with all our children. In essence, what they had to do was to come to the point where they were willing to "emotionally adopt" these children into their hearts and lives. Even though Karl and I had made the commitment to take one another's children to be our own, it did not necessarily mean our devotion would automatically trickle down to the members of extended families. The decision to embrace our entire brood, not just those with a biological connection, would have to be a choice extended family members made all on their own. *I have come to believe that this one decision ultimately determines the course and destiny of these relationships.* A rejection of this equality principle will doom these family members to a lifetime of emotional strain.

Quite recently, my mother recalled a conversation we had had concerning this very issue shortly after Karl and I were married. Evidently, at the time, she wanted to buy savings bonds for her natural grandchildren but when she told me of her plans, I told her that if she was not willing to do the same for all the children, then I would ask that none of them receive any. She said to me, "Sharon, I can remember those words as clearly as if they were said yesterday. I am so glad you said what you did. Because of your insistence for equality and my own decision to be a grandmother to all, I now enjoy such a wonderful relationship with each of the kids. This would have never happened had I decided to play favorites."

It is crucial that each of your relatives realize the significant impact their behavior, whether verbal or non-verbal, has on your vulnerable offspring. You must help each of them understand how fragile your child's self-esteem is at this point in their lives and how easily it can be damaged by careless acts of favoritism. The tendency for extended family members to prefer the natural over the blended child seems to be an on-going struggle and must be diligently monitored, emotionally speaking, for possible "security" breaches. I need to warn you, my friend, watching your children withdraw to their room during a family gathering after hearing an insensitive remark that related to them or after being forced to listen to unending stories of days for which they were not a part can be one painful experience. I have shed many a tear over such incidents in my own life. I am forced to admit that there were even times when I harbored a grudge of resentment when I saw my children being deliberately hurt, overlooked or set aside.

In order to avoid "resentment build-up" in this area of blended life, you must address these issues with the appropriate parties in a straight-forward manner and in a timely fashion. Confrontations are definitely in order when relatives ignore your demands for equality and blatantly decide to play favorites. One last thought...even though the following suggestion truly parts company with a tradition of the past, I am once again going to strongly suggest you encourage your extended families not to refer to your children as their stepgrandchildren, stepniece or stepnephew. I guarantee you that the same type of polarization I referred to earlier will occur between these two parties. The word "step" reeks of the past and its use implies a resolve to live therein.

The desired closeness to which I have been referring throughout this chapter was best expressed by one of our children in a practice letter I recently found from days in the sixth grade. In it was written, "Have I ever told you about my grandmother. She's the best." This extended family member had received the highest compliment of all because behind those words came the heartfelt sentiment, "God made a good choice by putting us together!"

Chapter 13

Work As If It All
Depends On You

*"We all love you very much. Thanks for
sticking it through for us. We know it
must be trying at times. You're always
there for us."*

Our children

It has been my desire throughout this book to
provide you with an honest, upfront look at the real world
of blended families. My words have been carefully
weighed as I sought to balance its unending challenges
with the potential fulfillment these unique relationships
offer. I believe deeply in the counsel I have offered you
because of its unifying effect on my own home. These
principles do work. They do facilitate the bonding
process. In fact, just recently I received a call from a
man in New Hampshire asking me to give a seminar in
his area because as he put it, "The best week I have ever
had with my stepson was the week after I went to your
workshop." The message he had heard directly influ-
enced his life so much that he wanted to expose other
struggling families in his community with its unlimited

possibilities. What did he hear that made such a difference? Was it the use of better communication skills? Was it a renewed sensitivity toward discipline? Was it the establishment of new family traditions? — possibly, but I don't think so. You see, as valuable as these truths may be, when they stand alone, they will always fall short of a complete solution to the complicated issues facing blended families.

What this man heard was a plan of action that was capable of changing not only his own behavior but that of his son as well. It was a message in which human achievement is in partnership with divine intervention. In personal terms, this translates into a formula which combines the efforts of the parents with the power of the Living God. I call it the key to successful blending. THE BLENDED PARENT MUST WORK AS IF IT ALL DEPENDS ON THEM AND MUST PRAY AS IF IT ALL DEPENDS ON GOD. I will unveil, in this and the following chapter, why this powerful combination can be so far-reaching in dealing with the never-ending conflicts facing a blended family.

I would like to begin by defining the role of the blended parent. What is expected of them? Are they responsible for the quality of life within the home? Why must the blended parent work so hard? In order to proceed with this frank discussion, it must first be understood that blended parents are never privy to the kind of automatic approval granted biological parents at the time of birth. The relationships they must build with their new children must be dug from the trenches on up, with nothing other than mental, emotional, and physical hard labor. There are no short cuts in the blended lane.

The odometer of progress will only register with the distance of time and effort.

Unfortunately, this kind of effort is becoming as extinct as the dinosaur these days. Our society has been inundated with a mind-set that says intimacy can be experienced on the first date and success can be discovered overnight. Hear ye! Hear ye! Hear ye! This kind of thinking has no place, whatsoever, in a blended home. Its rationale could not be farther from the truth when mirrored against its overwhelming needs. In fact, the only operating procedure acceptable is that of double duty in all areas of blended life.

To say the role of the blended parent is a critical part of the bonding process is, to say the least, an understatement. I would even go as far as to say that a blended parent can literally make or break their new home. The quality of their efforts will establish the very foundation on which the new family will grow. The strength of their consistency and resolve will determine whether or not the family will flourish. Because of this awesome responsibility, it is imperative that a blended parent embrace a work ethic that goes above and beyond the call of duty and a sense of dedication that runs around the clock. Leadership must always reflect a high level of commitment as well as a strong degree of effort. Nothing less will do.

I know in my own life that there were days when winning the gold in the triathalon seemed easier than keeping up with the individual and corporate needs of my new family. The responsibilities were that rigorous — the job description that inexhaustible. It has the ability to spin the head of even the most organized and disciplined soul. Not only was I expected to wear the hats of a housekeeper, cook, laundress, nurse, tutor, chauffeur, psychologist, and referee all in the same day, but each role required a strong hand of diplomatic flexibility.

The blended world is not a place for the rigid or unyielding personality, nor is it for the demanding, meticulous type who has trouble making concessions. Since compromise is literally the buzz word of a blended family's existence, this individual would be miserable and would drive everyone around them crazy. I spoke recently with a woman who had married such a prototype. Her husband's refusal to bend on his expectation for "perfect order" in their new home was creating continuous havoc. Because of his "self-centered" attitude, he was continually at war with his two new sons, ages 15 and 17! This is not surprising, since we all know how clean and neat teenage boys (or for that matter, girls) can be! This man should have remained single rather than to have added turmoil to a family that had already had its share of domestic unrest. So who would be considered a good candidate for this commanding position? "Go with the flow" kind of people, that's who. These are adaptable, bendable, flexible, and accommodating individuals. For them, compromise is not an option but a standard part of everyday life.

As for the challenges facing a blended parent, the stream is steady. In fact, there are times when its demands threaten to sap even the strength held in reserve. I found this sentiment repeated over and over again in my journal. Words such as, *"I'm exceptionally tired these days — maybe because of my busy, busy schedule"*; *"at times I get frustrated that there is not enough time for each child as well as keeping my house in order,"* and, *"my free time is so limited — a lot of adjusting that way,"* were regular entries. Surviving the rigors of blended life calls for a backbone of persistence, patience, endurance, and good, old-fashioned, stick-to-itiveness.

Since these relationships must be built block by block and brick by brick, the process can be painstakingly slow, especially with the hundreds of variables thrown into its path. Let me give you an example of what I mean. As warm as my daughter, Amy, was to me after my remarriage, I always got the feeling that there was some sort of a wall between us. I never understood where it came from but I always knew when she put it up. That is until almost two years after Karl and I were married. She and I had gotten into a minor argument on the beach and when I pressed her to open up and share her feelings, she stood up, grabbed her things and stomped off in a major huff (my kids taught me that phrase...I like it!). When I returned to the cottage, I found an envelope on the kitchen table with my name on it. Though the note inside was short, it spoke volumes as to why she had erected her invisible wall. She wrote, "The reason I don't want to open up and let anyone in is cause I'm afraid of being hurt again. I know you have said many times you would never leave me but I think I put up a barrier as a safety in case you did. Then it wouldn't hurt as much as if I had really gotten to know you super duper well." For her, it was a question of trust. For me, it was earning the right to claim that trust.

Being the novice that I was, the only strategy I could think of that might bring her "wall a tumblin' down" was to concentrate all my efforts on discovering who my new daughter was, what she thought, and how she felt. In other words, I had to get involved in her world. I remember literally sitting for hours shooting the breeze with this young lady. These times were not scraps off my calendar but blocked out periods of *Prime Time with Mom.* It was during those one-on-one times that I was given the opportunity to not only hear about her needs, but also how best I could address them. These were the moments when tears as well as laughter became a comfortable part of our relationship. Let me be honest ...relating with a child in this way can be emotionally and physically exhausting, but it is absolutely essential if you ever want to be considered one of their parents and not their mother's husband or their father's wife. The luxury of hindsight has helped me see the direct correlation between the amount of interest I showed and the amount of openness she offered. She needed to be enveloped with feelings of kindness, support, and love before she would begin to trust again.

In preparation for this chapter, I scanned many of the calendars I have kept over the past twelve years. I was amazed I was still alive! My husband and I didn't just dip our feet in the blended waters, we dove head-first... *Yikes!* Keeping up with the schedules of five very different and active children was an inexhaustible labor of love. Their interests were extremely varied and their energy levels tireless. Their individual schedules and their collective calendars sometimes made me dizzy. There were days on my calendars that recorded such entries as: Katy — cheerleading 2-4; Amy — basketball 3-5; Brian — intramurals 3-4; Rachel and Christy — swim lessons 4-5; Brian — basketball 7-8; and Rachel and

Christy — Awana 6-8. No kidding! Their extra-curricular sports programs included soccer, baseball, football, softball, karate, ice skating, basketball, tennis, swimming, and gymnastics. We often had more than one involved in the same sport but on different teams and there were days when we made six trips to the school or fields to keep up with the various practice and game schedules.

You can now understand why I could only find the words "Quiet Day...Hurrah!" twice on all the calendars I've kept since we were married. For the record, they were April 21, 1985 and October 25, 1988. I am putting them in print because if our children ever begin to question our effort on their behalf, these two dates will bring them to the inescapable conclusion that *they owe us big*! And this doesn't even include the number of school activities they were involved in such as play productions, marching band, chorus, science fairs, fund-raisers, and the duties of a class officer. When I say plays, I mean everything from "Benjamin Franklin" and "The Wizard of Oz" to "A Christmas Carol" and the "Hobbit". I kept the florist in business during those years with "Break a Leg" bouquets, not to mention the recitals, semi-formals, proms, and pageants they attended. There are so many long and short gowns in our closets that we are considering starting a rental shop for used formal wear. Finally, coupled with all of this were their church activities such as Awana, Boys Brigade, Youth Group, and "Kids Praise" musicals. Life for the Andersons would include everything from braces to blueberry picking.

People were always asking me how I did it all! At times, I really wasn't sure, but I did know how deeply committed I was to making my children's lives as full as possible while providing the security they so desperately needed. A standing joke around our house was that, "Mom doesn't even have enough time to shave her legs." Now that's busy!

I know one thing for sure...I never understood when I married Karl what I would be called upon to do for the sake of our new family. I had no clue how hard I was going to have to work before I would be able to see even a hint of camaraderie among the members of our family. It took such diligence to deal with the many complications that arose from bringing together two distinct families. I learned that blended parents can seldom "wing" their way through a day or, for that matter, even through an hour. There always needed to be a willingness to engage in legwork for the future. I never imagined having to make so many conscious decisions not only about my children's behavior, but about mine as well. Reacting and interacting in my home was like playing a game of Battleship, each move weighed and calculated. Even when I was forced to make off-the-cuff decisions, factors which I would have normally never considered had to be taken into account for the sake of peace on the home front. If you are reading this and are already part of a blended family, you have, no doubt, already said "Amen" after reading this paragraph. Or if you are about to enter this unique area of family life, you may be saying to yourself that it couldn't possibly be this much work. Well, it is!

What does it really mean to be a blended parent? Let the eyes of my journal mirror just a few of its implications. It means nurturing seeds of love when they break through the soil of resistance. It means overlooking childhood obnoxiousness by trying to understand the reasons behind the behavior. It means affirming a fledgling self-esteem when the world has been less than kind. It means promoting a sense of well-being for children reeling from pangs of social adjustment. It means remaining a strong and steady anchor in the unpredictable sea of life.

Lest I leave you with the impression that I was in there plugging away on my own, this was definitely not the case. The bulk of the domestic and child-rearing responsibilities was mainly mine because at the time of our marriage, I had chosen to be a full-time wife and mother. Though my husband's manufacturing business put tremendous demands on his time, he never made me feel our home was my sole responsibility. He made himself available to me as much as possible by providing a shoulder to cry on or a child to be taxied. We were team players — each giving 100% of who we were for the good of the team. He folded laundry, vacuumed rooms, and did dishes. I raked the lawn, planted the flowers and, one time, even helped roof the house. A blended home will never be successful if the physical, emotional, or mental load is distributed unevenly between the parents.

Genuine progress can only be realized when both parents are willing to embrace the words responsibility, diligence and sacrifice. The relationship they build with each other should not only be built on love but also on mutual respect and a joint resolve to "work as if it all depends on them". During our early years together, our children were not able to truly appreciate the love and energy expended on their behalf, mainly because of their age, but as they became older, they were able to see more clearly how deeply those lines of commitment and love ran. Just four years ago I received a card from my daughter, Katy, which said, "I feel I am beginning to see the flowers of the seeds you planted in my life years ago...I feel privileged to be able to grow with you not just as mother and daughter but as friends". I am so glad I never gave up on that relationship (and this young lady gave me one run for my money!). My daughter, Rachel, just recently wrote on her Mother's Day card, "My home is where you are because of all the love, joy and support you have given me over the years...you have been my guiding light...I don't think there has ever been another person who has made such an impact on my life." Other notes I have received included such words of gratitude such as:

> *"Thank you for all the individual time you spend with me"*

> *"I want to take time out to tell you what a great job you're doing — I can't believe all you do — it makes me proud to be your daughter"*

> *"Thanks for hanging in there with us"*

> *"Thank you for caring about my feelings — if I feel good or bad"*

"I'm so glad we have such a good relation-ship. Thanks for loving and caring for me"

"Thanks for all you do so often with no thanks"

These words have become as priceless to me as gold. I offer them not as a way of building myself up but in order to show you once again what can happen when a blended parent works as if the success of the family totally depends on their efforts while at the same time acknowledging, through prayer, that God is the only One capable of authentically bonding their precious family.

An anonymous piece I found years ago in a local newspaper sums up what I think should be the goal of every blended parent. As you work toward achieving wholeness as a family unit, seek to create a "Safe Place" for all its members.

In a safe place people are kind. Sarcasm, fighting, backbiting and name-calling are exceptions. Kindness, consideration, and forgiveness are the usual way of life.

In a safe place there is laughter. Not just the canned laughter of television, but the real laughter that comes from sharing meaningful work and play.

In a safe place there are rules. The rules are few and fair, and are made by the

151

people who live and work there, including the children.

In a safe place people listen to one another. They care about one another and show that they do.

Chapter 14

Pray As If It All Depends On God

To kneel and pray is nothing...unless I have also learned to walk and pray.

It is important for me personally to begin and end this book with praise and thanksgiving to God for the way He has answered our prayers, provided for our needs, and brought into our home the undeniable scent of love. If you remember in the introduction I wrote, "It is my honest conviction that we would have never been able to blend our families as well as we have without the help of God. He is truly in the business of bringing healing and wholeness into our daily lives. If I believe one thing about the past twelve years, it is this: Our God is a God of new beginnings. We have experienced His touch in our home and you can in yours as well."

These words were a direct result of a divine appointment God had made for me in the Fall of 1990. I had received a call from a women's group in the

Northeast asking me to give a workshop on Divorce, Solo-parenting, and Blended Families at their fall retreat. I was extremely reluctant to even consider such an invitation since I had gone to great lengths to keep our novel family out of the public eye.

We had undergone a great deal of scrutiny from the outside world, and I had no desire to bring further attention to our homestead. The years had made me very guarded as to what and with whom I would share the specifics of our family struggles. But after talking it over with a number of trusted family and friends, I decided to participate as a means of ministering to others who may be struggling in this area of family life.

I remember wondering why they were even offering such an elective at a Christian retreat and was certain there wouldn't be anymore than ten women in attendance. Little did I know then what a great need there was to address these issues, even in Christian circles, or maybe I should say, especially in Christian circles. Much to my amazement, over seventy women gathered for what would be an hour and a half of laughter and tears.

I shall never forget the face of a lady seated in the front row, who raised her hand as I finished and said, "After listening to you today, I now realize how many mistakes I have made." As tears flooded her eyes, she said, "Is there any hope for me?" Her piercing question touched me deeply, not as a speaker but as one who had, no doubt, made similar mistakes. I, too, began to cry. Somehow I remember answering, "If all I have talked about today was based on man's solutions, then I guess there would be little hope for you. But the words I have shared have been based on the Living God's power to change people and their situations and, for that reason alone, there is always hope."

These women seemed to bask in the openness of that forum. As one woman put it, "This is the first time a workshop such as this has ever been offered to us. So many times we are made to feel like our problems do not exist. We need to be able to talk openly about the struggles we face as well as be given the opportunity to learn positive ways of making the relationships in our homes better. You have done this for us today. Thank you for coming." Up until that weekend, I had wanted to hide the fact that we were a blended family, but now I knew, I could remain silent no longer.

God had spent the past twelve years teaching me a truth that desperately needed to be relayed to the blended world — *God is the only one who is able to make meaningful and lasting changes in a blended home.* This conviction had been formed within me as I watched Him dramatically change the complexion of my own home. My family is living proof of His transforming power. In fact, it boggles my mind to see the way He has smoothed the rough edges of our existence. Over the past decade, we have watched Him take the stench of dissension and replace it with an aroma of unity. We have seen Him carry our children through the valley of rejection and bring them to the summit of acceptance. We have experienced first hand His hand print of love on the relationships within our home.

The reason I have become so passionate about God's role in this emotionally charged environment stems from the fact that God is the only one who makes inward

155

changes in people's lives and most, if not all, of the conflicts and adjustments within a blended home are happening on the *inside* of its family members. The struggles they confront daily are happening within the very fibers of their heart, soul, and mind.

By means of an example, let me bring you back to a dark moment in our home years ago when Brian and Rachel first began their on-going feud. The argument they were involved in still remains a fog to me but the way it ended continues to be an inextinguishable memory. During those few short minutes, they managed to blame each other for everything including World War III! It ended with Brian running from the room screaming the words, "I hate you". Poor Rachel became a living example of the term the "walking wounded".

I tried my best to convince this young man how hurtful his words had been not only to his sister but to our entire family. His look of hostility, however, told me there was little I could do or say that would change his mind or alter his feelings. I learned a very important truth about blended life that day. You cannot make a child love a new parent. You cannot make brothers and sisters bond with each other. All the parenting skills in the world couldn't *make* Brian love Rachel or vice-versa. None of us have that kind of power — only God. Only the Creator has the power to make structural changes to the created.

Now in case you may be thinking I am some kind of emotional wimp who expects God to do all the rowing in the blended boat of life, you are wrong. I am a strong-willed woman by nature, almost dogged in my resolve and always ready for a new challenge. But I am also realistic. I know when I am in over my head. I know when I don't have what it takes. I know my limitations. And I knew from the onset of blended life that character alone would not be enough to withstand its bumps and bruises.

I quickly became aware of my need for a power greater than myself. Someone who could provide me with inner strength when emotionally drowning became more than just a passing thought. Someone who could heal my frayed and bleeding heart when it was systematically pierced with cutting remarks. Someone who could do for me what was humanly impossible. Someone who could change me and the members of my family from the inside out.

It was at this point where I discovered how prayer can significantly impact a blended home. I learned, as the old phrase goes, that prayer is not a substitute for working, thinking, watching, suffering, and giving, but it is a support for all these efforts. *If you take prayer out of the equation, a blended family will realize only limited and marginal change. They will never come to realize their full potential.* Soon after my son returned from working at a Christian camp a few years ago, I found crumpled in his footlocker the following piece on prayer.

"There is one sure test of prayer; no man can honestly engage in it and stay the way he is. His will strengthened; his pride humbled, his temper softened, his selfishness lessened, his love broadened and his courage increased. If he really prays, he will be changed. Prayer prompts forgive-

ness, sparks gratitude, overcomes tempta-
tion, turns ashes of defeat into flowers of
victory and fashions out of suffering the
fragrance of triumphant love. Prayer is
always changing things, never content with
what is negative, hopeless or lost; always
seeking to transform, to enrich, to create.
Prayer can become the most constructive
force in your life. "

Think what this could mean to the members of a
blended family. It would mean growth in relationships.
It would mean strength for everyday trials. It would
mean a broadened sense of love for a blended child. It
would mean unflinching courage for a blended mother.
It would mean a softened temper for a blended father. It
would mean positive and constructive change and lots of
it!

Time and time again my journal confirms the
influence my prayer life has had on me, my husband, and
our children. Most of the requests I recorded during our
early years together centered around the development of
love in our relationships. Regularly occurring were such
heart cries as:

> *"My prayer is that I would love them as if
> they were my own"*

> *"My prayer is that my love for him grows
> even deeper and that our relationship will
> only get better"*

158

"I pray deeply for a great love to be found between them. I know God is going to do a good thing there"

"I pray that we get closer"

In essence, I was asking God to make direct deposits of love to our attachment-starved hearts, to provide us with a sense of concern and rapport that He alone could give.

Another petition I continually brought before the Lord was our family's need for inner healing. After all, we had all known brokenness — Karl and I from a marriage; our children from broken homes. "Father, please heal us from within" I would ask, "mend the deep crevices of our hearts as only you can". This became a prayer I prayed for many years. I was convinced that unless we were engaged in a process of healing from the pain of our past, we would constantly be derailed on our journey toward building a new home life.

As I persistently prayed for this transformation, I watched, sometimes with wonder, how God's skillful hand created a simple landscape of growth and change on the canvas of our life. So it is not surprising to hear people tell us that unless you know the history of our family before you meet us, you would never know we were a blended family. The tie is that strong! *My friend, God answers prayer.*

Now mind you, this did not happen overnight. And it didn't happen with general prayers like "God bless our family". It happened when I made *specific prayers*; such as, "Father, my son is having a hard time adjusting to our new family. And since you know how best to change his heart, please do your work in his life. Give him a deep love for his new Dad and sisters." This was yet another prayer I prayed for many years. Little by little, there seemed to be a real softening in this young man's attitude. His sense of alienation was replaced with a sense of affection. The older he got, the more he seemed to appreciate the family he had and the efforts we had made on his behalf. To see the distance we have travelled, you would have had to be in our home recently when this 6'2" dynamo came home as a surprise visit from college. No, he didn't need money. Yes, he did have laundry. But he came home because as he put it, "I wanted to see my family...I was homesick". *My friend, God answers prayer.*

I was saddened to find at a seminar I did recently how few people actually viewed prayer as the ultimate catalyst of change for their blended home. So I was thrilled when at the end of the day, one of the participants came up to me and said, "If I leave here today with only one thing I have learned, it is to trust God, through prayer, to work out the difficulties we are facing as a family." She walked away with the key toward finding meaningful and lasting change in her home.

Are you praying specifically for the needs of your family? Are you praying consistently? *The health and welfare of your family depends on your faithfulness in this area. There is nothing you can do for your family that will have more value than bringing them before the Lord in prayer.* Pray when you become sensitive to the way your spouse disciplines your child; pray when you feel threatened by your child's other parent; pray when the responsibility of blended life seems too great; pray when you are in danger of emotionally abandoning your new family and pray when what little love you have is routinely tested by insecure and insensitive children.

Pray when your new child reminds you incessantly that they are not your child; pray when Christian people don't seem to want to accept your new family; pray when you feel your children are trying to put a wedge between you and your spouse. *Learn to take the rejection of a child and lay it at the feet of Jesus. Get in the habit of grabbing hold of His garment and allowing His power to flow through you when your emotional banks are on empty. Please remember, though, that this is a process. God will do His work but it will be done in His time and in His way.*

In closing, let me share with you a specific answer to a prayer I made years ago that made a profound impact on my life. As you know from past chapters, Katy, my oldest daughter, had a tremendous struggle with my role as her mother and often reminded me that she just couldn't call me "Mom". I prayed earnestly that "God would help me love her as if she were mine from the beginning of her young life," and committed myself to being as patient as possible with this hurting teenager. My prayers never ended nor my efforts ever waned.

Katy was due to go on her first high school retreat so we spent hours the night before she left packing all she would need (when you are that age, you pack ten sets of clothes for two days). It was late when we finished and as we parted in the kitchen, I said, "Goodnight, Kate" and headed for my room. As I reached the stairs, I heard her call out for the first time, "I love you, Mom". You will never know what those few words meant to me! As tears welled up in my eyes, I responded, "I love you, too". When I finally reached my room, I cried like a baby. It had been a long road but when I heard those few, simple words, it had been worth it all. I believe with all my heart that when you work and pray, God allows you to become partners with Him in the working of miracles. You see, "I love you, Mom" was a miracle!

Epilogue

The Arrival
of Bradley

Karl and I considered extending our family after we were first married but came to a quiçk conclusion that the addition of yet another human being in our home would have either killed us or put us into early retirement! You see, we were now at the point where we could finally sleep through Saturday morning cartoons, we no longer had to leap over gates in order to get from one room to another, and we finally could go just about anywhere as a family without a playpen, stroller, or diapers. After all, our youngest was five years old and we were just beginning to savor life outside the nursery. The case for "more life" was closed as far as we were concerned.

That was until December of 1986 when my gynecologist confirmed my female suspicion that I was indeed going to have a baby. It had been ten years since I had passed the rabbit test. My initial reaction of shock and apprehension soon gave way to exhilaration as I recalled once again what it meant to give life, to embrace the miracle of birth. Karl couldn't have been happier and was anxious to tell the world. The children were ecstatic and very surprised. Our greatest hope, of course, was that it would be healthy and that it would be a boy for Brian. After living in an all-girl house for the past five years, he deserved the "hero worship" a younger brother would offer.

After three months of looking "green around the gills", I began to enjoy the role of a lady-in-waiting. Bedtime came a lot earlier each night as I tried to keep up with the already busy schedules of a fourth-, fifth-, sixth-, tenth-, and twelfth-grader. Highlights of those nine months included a wonderful week at Disney World where I was denied entrance to such thrilling rides as "Space Mountain" (I should have read the warning signs); a delightful shower given by family and friends which replaced all the essential baby paraphernalia we had sold in yard sales years ago; and our first high school graduation where I was the *only* mother eight months pregnant!

Two days before I delivered, Amy and I were in an early morning car accident. The other driver had fallen asleep at the wheel. The police and ambulance felt a hospital visit was necessary but I felt a quiet day by the pool was in order. Since I am known for "spontaneous deliveries", it was no surprise to us that we arrived at the maternity ward just in time for me to deliver. The "birthing room" turned out to be a wonderful experience for our family since the children were permitted entry as soon as mother and baby were presentable (the only one missing was Brian who was away at camp). How thrilled we were as a family! It was as if a "Crown Prince" had been born. It was during those moments our family became keenly aware that this "surprise package" had been sent as a wonderful gift from God. You see, Bradley Karl Anderson *belonged to each one of us!*

Bibliography

Chapter 1

1. Charles E. Hummel, Tyranny of the Urgent (Downers Grove, IL: Intervarsity Press, 1967), P. 4

Chapter 2

1. Darlene McRoberts, Second Marriage (Minneapolis, MN: Augsburg Publishing House, 1978), P. 105

Chapter 7

1. Joyce Landorf Heatherley, Changepoints (Old Tappen, NJ: Fleming H. Revell Co., 1981), P. 75

Chapter 9

1. David D. Burns, M.D., Feeling Good—The New Mood Therapy (New York, NY: New American Library, 1981), P. 178

Chapter 11

1. Joyce Landorf Heatherley, Unworld People (San Francisco, CA: Harper & Row Publishers, 1987), P. 112

2. W.E. Vine, Merrill F. Unger, William White, Jr., Vine's Expository Dictionary of Biblical Words (Nashville, TN: Thomas Nelson Publishers, 1985), P. 382

Order Form

Bridges of **Hope**

MINISTRIES

Available now:

Book — "And the Two Became One Plus — An' Upfront Look at Today's Blended Family" ($11.95) by Sharon Anderson

Tape — "Bridges of Hope — Blended Family Seminar" Speaker - Sharon Anderson ($7.95)

Fill out this form and mail it along with a check or money order.

Please send me:

_____ copies of the book, "And the Two Became One Plus" by Sharon Anderson @ $11.95 each (plus $2.50 S&H per book)

_____ copies of the "Bridges of Hope — Blended Family Seminar" tape @ $7.95 each (plus $1.50 S&H per tape)

* * * * * * * * * * * * * * * * *

Please mail orders to:

Bridges of Hope Ministries
P.O. Box 407
So. Easton, MA 02375

or call:
(508) 583-1555

Notes

Notes

Notes

Notes